The Tiny Red
Bathing Suit of Mr. July

Inspiration & Resources for
Continuing Care Providers

Jean Clayton

THE
TINY RED
BATHING
SUIT
OF
MR. JULY

Inspiration & Resources for Continuing Care Providers

WOOD
LAKE
BOOKS

Editor: Jim Taylor
Cover design: Lois Huey-Heck
Consulting art director: Robert MacDonald

At Wood Lake Books, *we practice what we publish,*
guided by a concern for fairness, justice, and equal opportunity
in all of our relationships with employees and customers.

Canadian Cataloguing in Publication Data

Clayton, Jean, 1941 -
    The tiny red bathing suit of Mr. July

    Includes index.
    ISBN 1-55145-246-4

    1. Chronically ill–Pastoral counselling of. 2. Aged–Pastoral counsel-
ling of. 3. Pastoral care of the handicapped. 4. Chaplains, Hospital. I Title.
BV4435.C53 1997   259'.416   C97-910044-5

Printing 10 9 8 7 6 5 4 3 2 1
Published by Wood Lake Books Inc.

WOOD
LAKE
BOOKS

10162 Newene Rd., Winfied, BC,   Printed in Canada by
Canada V4V 1R2   Best Book Manufacturers

To my children
Jim, Jeff, Jenny and Joy
and
to my parents.

Table of Contents

Appendix

Information about diseases, illnesses, and disabilities

Worship services

Worship resources

General resources

Preface

"All great problems call for great love."
– Karl A. Menninger

A continuing care hospital (also called a long-term care or chronic care facility, home for the aged, or nursing home) ideally seeks to provide as full a life as possible for residents who require various degrees of medical support. In our financially-distressed times, those admitted to continuing care now are often those most in need of care, the very elderly frail or demented. Because of the irrational and deep-seated fears of old age and infirmity that many of us find within ourselves, pastoral care to this group can be daunting.

Many of the other residents of continuing care facilities are neither old nor demented, but have become physically unable to care for themselves any longer in the community because of illnesses such as Multiple Sclerosis, Parkinson's Disease, head injuries as the result of accidents, or other conditions and diseases. Young enough and clear enough in their minds to resent having to live in an institution, they present challenges of other kinds.

A Nine-Year Learning Experience

For nine years I worked as a chaplain in a continuing care hospital. It was one long learning experience. There were wordless lessons in courage or honesty. There were jolting reminders to me about loving my children well now, so that they might love me when I am old. I learned that there are many other ways of communicating beyond those to which I had limited my thinking, and I came to understand better how we are all affected by and deal with the inevitable experience of loss.

From these residents, I learned about the enormous variety of perspectives, religious and otherwise, that it is possible to bring to old age and to life-limiting illness. From their families, I learned much about faithfulness, fatigue, and frustration. From their caregivers I learned again and again that kindness is the best medicine. I learned that a gentle touch, combined with professional skill, could warm those cared for right to their souls and could heal. By contrast, perfunctory, grudging or impersonal care was blighting and life-draining. Although we are all always at the mercy of one another, this is most poignantly true when one is fragile and in need of help, and the other person is healthy and in a hurry.

I learned, too, to endure the deaths of many people who had become friends. Naturally, some relationships were deeper than others. When Carlie, an intensely maternal Dutch woman with a wall full of photos, died after many years of Multiple Sclerosis, I never walked by "her" room afterwards without a pang.

The Differing Demands of Chaplaincies

As I write this book, there does not seem to be a great deal in the non-scientific literature specifically about working with the old or chronically ill. Chaplaincy training as it stands tends often to focus on the crises of acute care. The crises of continuing care are less easily recognized as crises. They often take place in slow motion – the angst without the adrenalin.

Most continuing care residents are dealing with many losses, many changes. They grieve not only their physical and material losses, but the fact that their condition will probably eventually lead to death. They know it, and you know it. You must meet day after day after day with that knowledge as a part of your relationship, but not as its focus. Skillful and knowledgeable chaplains have their work cut out for them here, though the pace often calls for a different kind of energy from conventional chaplaincies.

Chaplaincy in continuing care is hard work. Because of the slower pace, that is not always as obvious as it would be in a palliative care setting, for instance, where the stress is more overt. But the stress of working with the dying and grieving is there, along with the challenge of supporting those who must live under difficult personal circumstances.

Chaplains in this setting, like chaplains anywhere, need to provide for consistent self-care to avoid burnout. Many of us have learned the hard way just how essential that is. For those blessed innocents who are not even sure what self-care is, it is a sort of balanced diet of the psyche. Play, as well as work. Pleasure, as well as dedication. A hobby, perhaps. Movies. Reading. Walking. Fun. For those who were so conditioned against selfishness that they shy away from the "self" part of self-care, it may help to think of self-care as a responsibility!

It is also true that the structure of pastoral care within institutions is itself in flux. Chaplaincy is being cut back along with other vital services. Community clergy and lay visitors find themselves being asked to provide more and more spiritual support in environments that may feel strange or intimidating. It is my hope that this book may be something of a guide.

In order to share what I learned, I also must risk sharing what I would do differently if I had it to do all over again – which occasionally means revealing what I didn't do well, or failed to do at all. Even so, it is my hope that this book will make a contribution to a specialized – and very special – field of hospital ministry. It will not tell you all you have always wanted to know about anything, but it may open doors which will lead to other doors of discovery.

With gratitude and admiration, I dedicate it to "my" residents. You were the very best part of the job!

Chapter 1
Continuing Care Institutions

More Like a Jail

Few people come to continuing care willingly. Sometimes the trig-gering event is the sudden disaster of a cerebral-vascular accident, a stroke, leaving in its wake paralysis of body or mind – or some-times both. Sometimes, it is the long, slow crisis of a disease like Multiple Sclerosis or Parkinson's disease or Alzheimer's. Their fami-lies have coped as long as they can, yet still feel tremendous guilt when they must surrender their relative to institutional care.

Larry

One male resident, Larry, was a very bright, bitingly sarcastic, former physician. I had met him many years ago, although he did not remember me. He was an atheist, and I felt intimidated and full of self-doubt in his presence. He was also extremely unhappy in hospital. Because I had been asked by staff to support him, I persisted in my awkward visiting until we hit upon something I could do that he found helpful.

He asked me to read to him. His book of choice was a strange and very long science fiction story about dolphins and space travelers, all with embarrassingly unpronounceable names. Cer-tain scenes described various interspecies sexual escapades which I tried to hurry over, uncomfortably aware of the ironically raised eyebrows of various nurses. Larry would lie, eyes closed, listening. Occasionally he fell asleep, so that next time I would have to go over the same ground again.

Larry controlled each visit. Once or twice, in our brief pre-reading conversation, he permitted us to touch upon the pastoral or personal. I was glad I had found a way to make myself available to him. For the most part, though, we were just two people in the same small room, with a book for a bridge between us. But at least there was a bridge.

After a few months, Larry died. I am sure he was greatly relieved. As for me, I wrote a poem.

The Resident

I feel like
Jonah
in the
black
bleakness
of the
whale's
belly,
alive
but
unheard,
unseen.
This place
encloses
without
protecting.
No one
comes in,
and
I cannot
go out.
This place
is bigger
than
my needs.
I could
die
here.

Larry was one of the people I really missed.

Many losses

Continuing care residents have experienced many losses by the time they are admitted: health, independence, dignity, status, choice, employment, the spontaneous sexual expression of an intimate relationship, dreams, the private control of bodily functions, possessions, travel... Because their losses have been gradual and progressive, so, often, their grief has been gradual and unrecognized, which makes it harder to process.

On admission to hospital, there are further losses: privacy, their home environment, and, to a large degree, access to their family. They may be required to wear diapers and take laxatives or enemas on a regular basis. They may be moved from bed to wheelchair by being swung through the air on the canvas sling of a Hoyer lift. (One new resident was a concern to staff because she refused to get out of bed. Conversation revealed that she was terrified of the Hoyer lift, and this was the only way she was permitted to be "mobilized.") Residents may be given medication without discussion, including tranquilizers or sleeping medication. Their choice of meals may be limited or nonexistent. If they cannot feed themselves, they may be fed too quickly by too-busy staff, so that eating becomes stressful rather than pleasurable. They have to go to bed and get up at the convenience of others. They may or may not have a TV, radio or telephone available to them. They may have little or no influence on the temperature of their room, and must depend on the kindness and patience of others for almost everything. Having a cup of tea when the mood strikes, or getting up to watch Casablanca on TV and eat buttered toast when they can't fall asleep, becomes a wild and unlikely dream.

Small wonder that residents sometimes seek relief from reality in confusion, become demanding, or die soon afterwards. Hardest of all, they must sometimes hear that cheery and unimaginative lie, "This is your home now."

"Hotel, perhaps," I used to suggest euphemistically when this came up in conversation.

"More like jail," was often the reply. But certainly not a home.

For many people, admission to continuing care somehow signifies the end of life. And they are right – it is the end of life as they have known it. Even though that life may have had its own losses, there was freedom, and identity, and room for personal idiosyncrasy – like eating raisin pie for breakfast, or window-shopping, or talking for hours on the phone. There was a bit of a garden, and neighbors who remembered them when they were just starting out in life. There was room for all the souvenirs that mark the special events of a lifetime. And if they needed to cry sometimes, they could do it without having to answer a lot of questions...

Tough folks

Yet this is not a new experience. Often, the people who have to deal with so many losses are the same people who survived the Great Depression, at least one World War, and probably the loss of a spouse, a marriage, or a child. The move to continuing care can trigger echoes of the grief-pain of those losses, and that is normal.

It is also normal to have developed personal ways of coping. Story-telling, mulling over the loss in personal quiet time, finding some way to pursue a hobby or to be useful to others in this new environment, are all ways of coping that chaplaincy can try to recognize and support. These newcomers have had to develop their own survival philosophies. Most value and practice independence, although a few who have been part of a very dependent relationship may feel great distress at having to carry on alone.

It is a sad truth that some of those admitted to continuing care die within a short time. It's almost as if they have made a decision that this new life is *not* better than no life at all. Others, who have worked all their lives to grow up and maintain their independence, become overwhelmed by having to surrender control of their lives to the regimens of an institution; they may adapt by becoming childishly passive.

Bracing soul-medicine

Most, I think, meet this new trial with strength garnered over a lifetime of ups and downs. Still, they often long to tell their stories, and to be regarded with respect. They can go it alone if they must – they've done it before – but many are glad of the spiritual and human companionship chaplaincy can provide.

We talk a lot about compassion in chaplaincy. While compassion is doubtless a good thing, an essential thing, it can be confused with pity. Respect can be bracing soul-medicine. Respect can be expressed as simply as using Mr., Miss, or Mrs. when addressing a resident, until and unless we are asked to use a first name. Respect means treating a wheelchair like an extension of a resident's body, so that we touch it only for a good reason, and preferably with permission. Respect means tapping on a door to announce our presence, even if the door is propped open. It means getting ourselves down to eye level for conversation, but asking first if we may sit down, and saying "May I?" before picking up a family picture for a closer look. It means not calling anyone "Dearie." And it means remembering that we, too, might have our own wheelchairs, someday.

A chaplain's assets

The most useful asset of any chaplain is surely a well-tuned imagination. With it, we can put ourselves in the position of the one we are visiting without being overwhelmed. In a word, empathy.

Another "must-have" asset seldom mentioned in training is a sense of humor. When I ended up, as I often did, torturing my stiff knees by squatting next to a resident's wheelchair so that we could have conversation eye-to-eye, or shouting a prayer into almost-deaf ears in spite of the skeptical amusement of a nearby nurse, it was clear to me that personal dignity had better not be my main concern! And when I introduced myself for the 20th time to the same confused resident, I tried to remind myself that it was that moment that mattered, and not the past or the future.

Thanks to a two-year stay in a hospital during my teens because of tuberculosis of the kidney, I began chaplaincy with an advantage. I knew how it felt to be on the non-visiting side of the bed. I knew about feeling regimented, about long and boring evenings and weekends, about being homesick and the disproportionate importance of each mealtime. I knew, too, how a cold, impersonal caregiver could cast a pall over a day, and how a pleasant, warm nurse could brighten a day. I knew something about the politics of having room mates I did not choose, and about the embarrassment of using a bedpan in a four-bed ward with visitors in the room and ringing in vain for someone to take it away.

And I had experienced the deaths of fellow residents. I knew that a hospital was never "home." Yet for a time it necessarily became my world.

Theology and continuing care

Continuing care, like good theology, is a matter of the present moment. The past enters into it, as unfinished business which might need to be revisited in the here and now, or as memories which inform or nourish it. As for the future, no one is more aware of the fact that we all walk on thin ice than the continuing care resident. But what matters is today's food, today's comfort, today's visitors. We meet one another where we are, and focus mostly on today.

It is those stories I shall tell in this book.

I shall of course respect the privacy of the residents I worked with by disguising their names. The hospital itself was part of a Roman Catholic institution which also included an acute-care hospital and a home for the aged. Although certain expectations and prejudices existed for ministry because the institution was Roman Catholic, many of the residents were of other denominations. A few were of other faiths.

Part of my job was to coordinate the weekly ecumenical worship service. Over time, this task coordinated my own Roman Catholic spirituality into something more ecumenical. Although this new perspective was sometimes confusing to others on staff, it seems to me to be a good thing. Certainly, I developed (and retain) a strong sense of us all journeying in the same direction, whatever our religious language or taste in symbols.

I wish I could introduce you to every one of the residents I remember. I do intend to have you meet some of them – or people who represent them – through stories I wrote at various times during my time at the place I will call St. Mary's. The stories will help you and me, together, to look at several key areas in continuing care chaplaincy: support, worship, communication, crisis, and integration through life review.

Let's begin with Benny and Simone.

Chapter 2
Worship services

The intoxication of the Sign of Peace

"Do you like bingo?" asks Benny, slowly.

It is his standard question to all visitors, and I am never sure of the correct answer, although I have tried them all: yes, no, sometimes. Perhaps there isn't a correct answer.

Benny is fascinated by a game that he can't see. He is also much taken with Texas, which he has heard about in Westerns read to him by a volunteer. He will never see Texas, either. Dr. Foster, he says, took out his eyes when he was a baby, 60 years ago. They were "ulcerated." Benny left the farm where his family lived to spend eight years in a school for blind children. Braille was hard, but he made friends there.

Now he spends all day in a wheelchair in a hospital for the chronically ill. But it's an improvement over the psychiatric hospital that used to be his home. He rocks himself, and sleeps a lot. He likes his meals, and sometimes laughs loudly for no reason I can see. Once in a while, one or another of his brothers comes to visit.

As we talk, I rub his back gently, touched by the way he relaxes and softens so unselfconsciously. I ask if he dreams, because I have sometimes wondered if and how blind people dream. Yes, indeed, says Benny, without saying more. Perhaps he dreams of lemon meringue pie, which he seldom gets any more, but he remembers that his mother used to make it. Now, he says, she is "making it for the angels." I'm not sure who told him that, but he seems to like the idea.

Later I visit Simone. She is sitting in a corner of the so-called sunroom. She is not happy today, and tells me earnestly that she is not crazy.

Someone has said something, and Simone is hurt. "I have a nice disposition," she says, perhaps quoting someone kinder. And she does. Simone is a lady, but she has trouble thinking in an ordinary way, and she knows it. But she's not crazy. She knows who she is and tells me again, using all three names. So I reintroduce myself, too, and explain in answer to her question (although we have met many times) that I'm "sort of a hospital minister."

"Are you!" exclaims Simone with polite interest. "I'm nobody!" she adds, and suddenly bursts into tears. This is a new thing in our visits; it distresses both of us. I affirm this lady who knows who she is, who is aware of her gifts and her difficulties.

Then, because I need to leave, I take her to the TV room where blind Benny sits alone, and park her wheelchair close to his. I make sure they know each other's names.

"How do you do?" asks Simone politely.

And Benny asks slowly, "Do you like bingo?"

A narrow and confining world

Like many residents, neither Benny nor Simone had many visitors, and little family. The hospital became their world. Yet it did not focus on them, but on routine and staffing, as is the way of an institution.

Conversation with Benny and Simone was not of the cocktail party variety. They were often sleepy, sometimes confused, sometimes – I suspect – deliberately seeking pleasanter places in memory or an altered state of consciousness.

Good chaplaincy training requires working without an agenda – thank God. I met Simone and Benny, and many like them, where they were. Sometimes where they were had little connection with what we think of as the real world. One day, Simone told me she had had 30 babies the previous month. Impressed, I asked her what she had done with them all. "Put them out to pasture," she replied, smiling with pleasure at her ingenuity. It certainly seemed like a good idea to me!

Renewing worship services

Both Simone and Benny enjoyed the regular Friday ecumenical services. Although hymn books were of no use to Benny, he had learned his favorite hymns by heart, and sang them loudly. Simone tended to carry on loud and unrelated conversations with those near her during chapel time, because she was at heart a social person. She enjoyed having a volunteer sit next to her, ostensibly to help her find the correct hymn, but really to take a special interest in her and help to meet her craving for connection.

For the Protestant crowd, Friday was our Sunday. Sunday morning itself was used for two Roman Catholic masses. And although we sometimes held a Sunday afternoon service for special occasions, afternoons were usually geared to napping or outside visitors, so the afternoon time did not work well. So we settled for Friday morning. We stuck with the same time and made sure services were regular. Worship leaders sometimes came from local churches; sometimes the services were led by staff chaplains or chaplaincy students. Volunteers helped bring residents to the chapel and escorted them back to their rooms.

I was painfully aware that these worship services often lacked life. When a chaplain at a nursing home wrote me to ask for advice on running her own services for Alzheimer's residents, I felt sufficiently embarrassed to try harder to understand what changes needed to be made to make these services meaningful for the residents.

One of the things that just seemed wrong to me was that the "wheelchair folk" formed a sort of island in the middle of the chapel, while those able to walk occupied the side pews. There wasn't a lot of singing from the "island."

As an experiment, I made sure that several folding chairs were set up in the chapel before each service began, and asked volunteers and students to occupy these chairs, so that they sat among those in wheelchairs. As well as being able to help them find their hymns and provide cues to those who were blind or confused, the presence of the volunteers provided a vital human connection, a feeling of church family that helped to balance any feeling of isolation or differentness. We made sure we had an organist at every service, provided large-print books of familiar hymns, and asked volunteers to sit near the door with residents who were especially restless or noisy.

The singing improved. So did the atmosphere.

Other changes also came along. We began to recognize the importance of the life-giving Sign of Peace, and asked all the worship leaders to incorporate it into every service after the Lord's Prayer. At the Sunday morning Catholic masses, I noticed how residents who seemed otherwise unaware of their surroundings responded to the Sign of Peace that was part of each mass. It struck me that Protestants, too, might avail themselves of this human sacrament of connection. Miraculously, it seemed, just as at mass, residents who seemed oblivious the rest of the time came alive when their hands were gently taken, their eyes looked into, and the gentle, simple blessing given: "Peace be with you." So intoxicating was this connection to all of us that the Sign of Peace was exchanged lavishly, every volunteer, student and chaplain making the rounds of the whole chapel. (Well, not *everyone* found it intoxicating. One genteel Presbyterian lady, Nettie, found it quite unseemly in the beginning. She extended her obvious disapproval with only the very tips of her fingers, and said in a loud voice to her neighbors that she had never seen anything like this in all her Presbyterian years. But even Nettie warmed up after a few months.)

Memories and meditations

The liveliest service we ever had was an "I Remember" service at which we sang hymns we all remembered from Sunday School long ago. We had fun that day. Reading, remembering, or just holding up a hymnbook was a problem for many residents. But many of them easily recalled these hymns, though we provided printed versions as well. Since memories come with feelings and associations attached to them, we had more than our share of youthful energy for that service.

Another effective service involved a simple meditation. Since I have seen this work with children of three and four as well as with worshipers like those at St. Mary's, I am convinced that human beings have a natural facility for this type of prayer, and wonder why it isn't used more consistently with "ordinary" congregations. Those present are asked to bring to mind (or sometimes to bring actual photos, but this takes advance preparation, and leaves out the visually impaired) a picture of someone they love. They then spend some time with that image, sending it love, or speaking words that they would like to say. Background music enhances the meditation. Very simple, yet profoundly touching and peaceful. Mother's Day or Father's Day is a good time for this idea, keeping in mind (and gently putting into words) the fact that not everyone present has or had a loving parent to remember. Sometimes the words need to be words of forgiveness, with acknowledgment that this is not an easy thing.

Concrete symbols

One Friday I brought in a brightly-striped afghan to drape over the altar. (I later found that Sister Sacristan was a bit shocked.) The afghan served as an audio-visual for the story of Joseph's ups and downs, as well as for reflecting on the bright and dark days and stories of those present. A patchwork quilt would serve the same purpose.

Audio-visual aids that can be seen, touched, smelled, or distributed are welcome, especially when they bring the lost outside world a little closer – autumn leaves, daffodils, lilacs, freshly-baked bread. Babies are also welcome, and my brand-new grandson came with his mother to a service at which I was definitely peripheral!

Remembrance Day was a very special day for this congregation. We distributed poppies and recited *In Flanders Fields*. Sometimes we were able to find an obliging bugle player. Although our congregation was largely female and may not have seen combat, they were glad to have their sacrifices remembered: bravely sending off to war beloved family members or spouses, rationing, rolling bandages or knitting socks for the Red Cross... Some had been in England during the war, and had their own tales to tell.

Frannie was one of these, a transplanted Englishwoman who still had nightmares of bomb shelters. Twice she had emerged from such shelters to find her house burned to the ground. Small wonder that she became depressed each time her room was changed within the hospital. She had other stories, too. I especially liked the one she told of bicycling desperately all over the neighborhood to find something to make a supper for her soldier husband, who was home on leave. She stole a turnip from a garden and begged a shopkeeper for twopence worth of cheese ends. She went home with these treasures, and, she told me, knelt down and prayed that she might somehow make a feast for her husband. She took some red cellophane paper and crumpled it into the fireplace. She said it was "almost as good as a real fire." "And do you know," she would say (for she told this story many times), "after dinner, my Len said it was the best meal he had ever tasted! There, now!"

Frannie would get teary on Remembrance Day, but she was glad that we did remember.

A typewritten note taped to the lectern by a blessed bygone priest forthrightly reminded all who preached there to "keep language inclusive." I was more than happy to comply, especially when the congregation was so largely female.

Worship leadership

For part of my time at St. Mary's, we had a student chaplaincy program led by a supervisor who very much valued and understood training in long-term care. She requested students to take turns leading these services, and then leading a theological reflection afterwards. I was given the task of orienting these students to our chapel protocol. I enjoyed working with students. In the orientation I used an article I had published in *The Journal of Pastoral Care*, (Summer

1991, Vol. XLV, no. 2), which is reprinted in the Appendix of Resources at the end of the book, along with a sample service.

Sometimes various community clergy would come to lead a service. This was appreciated, as it was done on a volunteer basis. I noticed that the congregation's favorites were usually gentle, older ministers. If, however, community clergy insisted on a cheerleading "Is everybody happy?" approach (possibly in reaction to the anxiety some of them felt at St. Mary's), they were not invited again. It felt false and alienating to me to ignore the pain and sadness some of the residents felt, or the disabilities many of them had to work around. It seemed to make more sense to acknowledge these facts-of-life occasionally, as part of life at St. Mary's. During worship, they were mentioned in context, together with faith and the reality of a loving God.

The last thing to go

My mother used to say that sexuality was "the last thing to go" as we age. Certainly loving touch seemed to quicken the pulse of the spirit.

The "new life" that I marveled at during the Sign of Peace or at communion time, even among extremely confused, very sensorially deprived persons, was also apparent whenever the local Anglican priest made his or her monthly bedside visits after celebrating the Eucharist. We were blessed with a small but faithful team from St. Paul's (Anglican) Cathedral. They appeared without fail on the third Tuesday of every month. After the service, I went with them to visit our bed-bound Anglicans. I remember being especially impressed by the alacrity with which one kindly dean always managed to sidestep Greg, an Anglican who no longer remembered anything about life except its sexual side, and who attempted to grab male visitors and caregivers, ordained or not, in quite a personal way. The dean leaped gracefully aside, without missing a beat in his blessing.

Almost all of those we visited were unable to receive communion, and indeed hardly seemed to be alive at times. And yet, when gently touched, the old words of a familiar blessing or of the Lord's Prayer seemed to cause a spark, a stirring. In those who were unable to attend chapel, but were still cognitively aware, the gratitude for this faithful visiting by a representative of a lifelong church was a touching reminder of its importance.

Ideas for reflection or group discussion

- ..... What place does touch have in worship? What touches you?
- ..... How do you feel about being touched? Touching? About touchy-feely people?
- ..... Role play a touch-healing miracle to see how it feels.
- ..... Take turns attending a service in your institution in a wheelchair. Put Vaseline on your glasses and/or wear earmuffs. How was it?
- ..... Use this idea as a role play, noticing your reaction to touch and attention when your other senses are muffled.

Chapter 3
Dementia

An old woman's sad song

*"From clinical observation we in fact do know that
brain-damaged persons are very susceptible to the atmosphere
in their environment and that their reactions
of an illuminated smile or a catastrophic anxiety response
can be triggered by tone of voice or touch."*

Miriam J. Hirschfeld, R.N., D.N.Sc.,
"Ethics and Care for the Elderly"

What is it like to suffer from the dementia that results from a stroke? (And how can anything so devastating and sudden be called a "stroke"?)

I often asked myself this question, and tried to listen carefully to those who were trying to tell me by their words or (more often) by their behavior what it was like, so that I might have a better idea of what was needed. I imagined myself as a confused old woman, trying to see my surroundings from this possible future point of view. One day I wrote this story.

Sarah

My name is Sarah. I think I am being held captive in this place. When I am in bed at night, there is a silver fence all around, so I can't get out. Once, I climbed out over the bottom of the bed, but I fell, and now they tie me in. When I sit up in a chair, there is a strap across my lap. But I wouldn't run away. I have no idea where I would go.

My name is Sarah. When I sing it to myself, weaving the notes into a sort of charm, I feel better. Sarah, *Saaa-a-rah*. If I sing it just so, and close my eyes, sometimes I can be in my swing, under the big tree, in the shady place. Gently at first, I swing. I can smell the geranium leaves crushed under my feet. I can hear the lazy bees, drowsy in the sun. I pretend my swing is a pendulum, and swing my legs, bend my body, until I am moving back, forward, back, forward, until I am flying, flying and singing, and the day is singing, too. The golden morning and the sun sing with me, Sarah, *Saaa-a-rah!* And then I come crashing down, and the angry voice is shattering the morning every which way. "Sarah! Stop yelling! Be quiet!" And I am back in the chair, in the long hall.

There are others here, too. They sit in their chairs in this long hall, but they don't talk. Sometimes I wonder about them, who brought them here. I can't really see them very well. I had glasses, but they got broken. But it's the strangest thing, when I close my eyes, I can see quite clearly. So I close my eyes, and soon I see my mother, and I can smell milk and powder. This time I am in her arms, looking up, and she looks down at me, all broody and warm, and rocks me, rocks me and sings, Sarah, *Saaa-a-rah*. And I sing in my head with her. I look up at her and she looks down at me, and we remember when we were even more together. First, I lived in her, and now she lives in me, in my head, in my heart. And we rock and sing.

When I feel a jerk and a bump and something being tied around my neck, I know I am back in that other world, the bad-dream world.

"Lunch, Sarah. Open your mouth."

They feed me, too fast, but they are in a hurry. It dribbles down my chin, and itches, but when I try to scratch the itch, I knock the spoon out of the nurse's hand by mistake. "Sarah! Watch what you're doing!"

I want to tell her I'm sorry, I didn't mean it. But I know from the way they act when I talk that it doesn't make sense to them. Anyway, the nurse isn't talking to me now, she is talking to another nurse feeding the old woman next to me. They are talking about their babies at home. I don't mind. I like to hear about the babies.

But after lunch, they wheel in that lifting machine. They hook it up to the canvas cloth under me, and swing me through the air into bed. It scares me, so I go to that safe place inside my head until it is over. Afterwards, the nurse changes me. I am dirty, and the diaper smells, and I close my eyes because I know there will be the tightening around the nurse's mouth that she can't help. I used to ask to be taken to the bathroom when I first came here, but they would tell me to go ahead and do it in my pants, because it took so long to get me up and back to bed. It was so hard to do that, so I would hold it and hold it until it exploded out, because then at least I would have tried, at least I wouldn't be doing it on purpose. But it smells so bad, and the nurse turns away her head. And I, too, try to get away from the smell.

This time, I am in the room I had when I was 17, the white and blue room with the pretty dressing table. There is lace on my underwear, and my cologne smells of flowers, and I powder myself with fragrant white dust. I slip, so clean, into sandals and a white dress, crisp and still warm from the iron, and open my window to the July evening. The scent of the roses rises up to persuade me to come outside, too, and the air is like warm silk. I run down the stairs, out to the porch where my mother and father sit rocking and Frank stands nervously. I laugh into his shy brown eyes, and he grins, and we say goodbye and run off to the dance. Frank holds me close to the music, and whispers into my hair, "You smell so good, Sarah."

And then it is that other world again, and time to wake up. Someone, Karen, the nice fat nurse with the slowness about her that gives me time to catch my breath, comes in. She changes me, and I'm not dirty this time. She is glad, and so am I. She turns on the TV. "Jody Stewart, from Gumball, Arkansas, come on DOWN!" yells the announcer, and this Jody gallops in from somewhere, breasts bouncing, and everyone screams.

Karen leaves with a smile. My roommate has gone to sit in the sun with her daughter. I am alone. A ray of sun leans across my bed, full of dancing dust. I look into it, and remember a winter childhood evening, lying in the snow under a streetlight, looking up at a world full of whirling snowflakes and light, pretending I was in one of those glass globes full of water and white flakes.

And then the door opens, and a sandy-haired man and a woman come in and stand by my bed. "Mom," says the man, "how are you?" He looks sad.

The woman, pretty for her age, but colder than the snow, stares at me. "Don't you remember us? John, she doesn't remember us." She sounds a little bit joking and a little bit offended. So I try to smile, but only one side of my mouth twitches. Then, all at once, I want to laugh, so I do. They look at each other, shocked, and then I feel so lonely in my laughing that before I know it there are tears on my face, catching on my wrinkles and trickling to my ears. Tears in my ears, I think, and laugh again.

"Labile," I hear Karen saying to them, and I realize she is talking about me. "It goes with a stroke. She's labile." It sounds rude, somehow. Soon, they go away. Karen takes a tissue and wipes my face. She strokes my hair back, turns off the TV, says "Sarah, shh. Rest." She goes away.

I close my eyes. The room is so still, I can hear my heart. It sounds loud, regular. I listen to the beat. Soon, I am the beat. It is like a drum, like wood being chopped, like love-making. I think of the tide, in, out, in, out. I think of rocking, of singing. I begin to sing. "Sarah, *Saaa-a-rah*." I sing and I rock. And someone comes and closes the door so I won't bother the others again.

"Let the old woman sing," I hear Karen say kindly enough, as the door swings shut. "At least she's happy."

I sing, louder and louder, all the stops out this time. Yes! My name is Sarah!

Imagination for caregivers

My name is not Sarah, of course – I couldn't bring myself to use my real name in that story, because that could feel too threatening. And no doubt I have romanticized Sarah's situation. As nice as it would be to easily slip into a warm or pleasant memory as a coping mechanism, the damage that a stroke inflicts on the brain might preclude control of this kind. Still, such exercises of imagination can at least help us to feel closer to a resident, to help bring about the kind of trust relationship that is the most useful thing we can offer to residents and to ourselves, and to be able to better empathize with the resident's family and caregivers.

Much of Sarah's story was just fact. The Sarah's and Sam's we meet often do have to wear diapers ("incontinence briefs"), be lifted in and out of bed, and sometimes be restrained. Safety – for both resident and caregiver – must be maintained, and time and energy have their limitations. As a chaplain I often felt I walked a tightrope between empathy for residents and understanding the realities of institutional life. I was always glad that "resident advocacy" was clearly named in my job description.

Alzheimer's disease

Sarah's dementia was the result of advanced Alzheimer's disease. Dementia, characterized by memory loss, disorientation, cognitive decline, and inappropriate social behavior usually progresses to the point where others must manage even the most simple physical activities for the resident.

Although Alzheimer's disease accounts for two-thirds of all dementia, there are other kinds. These include AIDS dementia, vascular dementia, alcoholic dementia, and dementia as the result of Parkinson's disease. Although the disease can progress to the point where the resident does not seem to be aware that he or she is suffering, family members often suffer more and more as the condition worsens. It must be a very sad and lonely thing not to be recognized by, for example, your mother or husband. It must be terribly hard to grieve the loss of someone who is still living, yet who has died in some ways.

According to the National Advisory Council on Aging, in 1991, 8% of Canadians 65 and over suffered from dementia, about 250,000 human beings. More than twice as many women as men were affected. About half of these seniors were living in an institutional setting. Among the institutionalized seniors with dementia, their family caregivers were most likely to be daughters, many of whom were already employed and/or with their own family responsibilities.

Some of the faithful next-of-kin were not actually kin at all, but long-time friends, and these also sometimes require support. One lovely woman who had been a university professor was visited every Wednesday afternoon by a former colleague. It was very good to see them together, because Lila's visitor obviously treated her as though she hadn't changed a bit, a true friend-of-the-heart.

Living with the Sarah's

As for the Sarah's, what did I do? What can we do? I asked this question of a colleague who had worked for several years in continuing care, a man of warm, pastoral presence. As well as working in this capacity professionally, he had lived the gradual progress of his own mother's Alzheimer's disease.

He told me of a recent visit with his mother, who no longer remembers who he is, but appreciates his visits because she likes him and realizes that he likes her. On this occasion, they sat in a waiting room together, as she had a medical appointment. She liked the color of a chair.

"Yes," he said. "It's nice, isn't it?"

They sat, looking at the chair, and for a minute or two, together in appreciation. He validated her feeling, and joined her in it, a tiny window of opportunity for the ministry of relationship, of connection. It's the radical opposite of writing off another person as demented, or too different to relate to, to communicate with. It's love, of the most peaceful, healing kind.

My friend also reminded me that there is still a place for laughter, even in the midst of the grief of seeing his mother drift further and further away from relationship with everything familiar, everyone beloved. He told of a visit to a restaurant where his mother had solved the problem of too-hot french fries by dipping each one carefully in her iced tea. He and his grown sisters looked at each other ruefully, and then laughed – with their mother, who was quite pleased with her solution.

Building relationships

Ministry in long-term care is nothing if not flexible, and what is that but practical creativity? Sometimes I fed a Sarah her lunch, after getting permission from the staff (some residents had difficulty swallowing and were at risk for asphyxiation). I took my time about it and tried not to let my own food preferences pass judgment on the green-and-brown pureed concoctions provided for dementia patients. As well as supporting busy staff, this always seemed to me a tender non-verbal way to demonstrate some basic caring to residents. It also helped keep me grounded in my job, reminding me that chaplaincy was about more than leading worship services. It was about a coming together of human needs, mine to give and others to be assisted...

It was relationship building, as sacred an activity as we are presented with. Their needs sometimes included a drink of water, putting a bedside table within reach, opening and/or reading a letter or card, and turning a TV or radio station on, off, or to a less toxic station than the ones playing the loud music that the young nurses often amused themselves with while they worked.

One elderly French resident loved to listen to a French station on her radio. But invariably, when I visited, the station would have been changed to some version of radio station ROCK. Pasting a reminder on the radio didn't seem to help. Eventually a sympathetic member of the maintenance staff adjusted the tuning mechanism so that it could not be moved from the French station. Blessed be his house.

Another resident, slow of mind, speechless, and with a severe salivation problem, preferred a classical station. She was able to convey this to a few interested persons. My customary ministry to

Brinna was a greeting, followed by finding her a dry spot on the towel beneath her chin. Then I turned off the TV soap it was assumed she would want to watch (and didn't like). I admired her newest stuffed toy, and turned her radio to the classical station she enjoyed. Sometimes I prayed with her, and for her – usually when she was unhappy. She was never more unhappy than when her husband suddenly died, and for a month or so wept soundlessly whenever I visited. She was unable to attend his funeral, so I arranged a mini-service at her bedside, along with a student chaplain.

Her life had been a difficult one, and she bore its many trials with a simple grace. After a month or so, we resumed our customary routine.

Working with a family in pain

Visiting family members of any resident appreciated seeing that such personal little gestures were offered. After noting them, they would seem more comfortable about talking with me. Most were timid about any complaints they might have. They invested heavily in staying "on the good side" of staff. They did not want to be considered difficult, and were glad just to be able to vent these concerns or worries to someone. Sometimes, I could help; always, I encouraged them to speak to staff or even to take their concern to the resident advocate if necessary.

I felt overall care was good in the facility, and could say so in good conscience. But with steadily reduced staffing and levels of training, problems did inevitably occur.

Even without these complications, most family members had some guilt and pain about bringing a loved one to live in an institution, which had nothing to do with the relative excellence of St. Mary's as a facility.

The very act of having to institutionalize a relative or spouse was often very difficult for a family member, even when the situation at home was clearly impossible to maintain and not in anyone's best interests any longer. Guilt and sorrow were often part of the package. Grief was always part of it, a natural reaction to the loss of the ordinary dream of growing old together or of continuing as a family. It often took weeks or months before family members could begin to find their way through the maze of hope and denial that is an inevitable part of such a situation. And since most of these families had cared at home for their relative until they could no longer do so, many were exhausted and even suffering from depression – which is twice as common in someone who cares for a dementia resident than in someone who cares for a person without dementia.

The time of admission to continuing care is a vulnerable time for whole families. Family support during these first weeks or months of adjustment seems an important part of useful chaplaincy, a consistent, accepting, listening presence. Normal feelings of anger and a fear of "selfish" feelings were often part of such conversations. When anger in this context was calmly acknowledged as a natural part of a loss experience, and when the threat of "selfish" feelings was declawed and seen as a normal desire to live as fully as possible, it seemed to help. Usually. For one or two people, their anger seemed as frightening as a black hole in space that, for them, led straight to hell.

Genetics plays a role in the risk of developing Alzheimer's. The chances of developing Alzheimer's increase by 2.5 times if you have a close relative with the disease. Family members sometimes were reluctant to visit, because seeing the resident reminded them of the possibility that they, too, might share the same fate.

Denying reality

Sometimes, too, family members clung so strongly to their recollection of the resident as a healthy person that they found it extremely difficult to relate to this apparent stranger as their father, mother, sister, husband, or wife. This was especially true if the change had been sudden, as with a stroke – just as bereavement through death is more difficult when it is sudden. Relatives occasionally pushed very hard for a rehabilitation placement, convinced that the ailing family member could be restored to his or her former self with enough exercise and therapy. Sometimes a physician would finally give in to this pressure. He or she would give the necessary order for rehabilitation to be attempted, even when it was obvious that nothing could reverse the damage that had occurred to the resident, just so that the family or spouse could see this reality for themselves.

A degree of peace often came with acceptance, but it was hard-won. Most were eventually able to make the adjustment. A few gradually disappeared, rationalizing that they wanted to "remember them as they were," sometimes even instituting divorce proceedings.

Sometimes, when a close relative died, I was asked to provide support to the bereaved resident. Reluctant to add to a resident's burdens, other family members sometimes tried to hide the bad news from the resident. Usually, though, the family could be persuaded to be honest about the death. They realized the tangle of misunderstanding and confusion that would result from being less than truthful in such a situation.

If the resident was unable to attend the funeral, I would try to find a way to help them participate. Once, I attended the funeral and brought back a tape. The resident was able to listen to it and find comfort in it. At other times, either alone or cooperatively with a student or staff member, after making arrangements with the resident and with staff, I offered a mini-version of a memorial service at the resident's bedside, at the same time the funeral itself was taking place.

Once, I took a candle to a resident's room to enhance such a service. I realized just in time that I had better not light it, since the resident was on oxygen...

Building bridges

Chaplains often function as connectors. They bridge for a resident the hospital world and the "outside." They bring news of the outside world directly, or they call a favorite priest or pastor for an occasional visit to maintain a link with a church from the past.

Sometimes the bridge is between resident and family or friends. A friend who works as a continuing care chaplain in another city is especially sensitive to the discomfort visitors sometimes have when first visiting someone like Sarah who is now very different from the person they once knew. This chaplain, Tina, accompanies such visitors. In her friendly, matter-of-fact way, she helps them to become reacquainted with the resident, answering any questions they might have, and modeling appropriate behavior for them until they become more comfortable. This is a great service to the resident as well as to any visitors. It could very well make the difference between withdrawing from the relationship and further visits.

What else can we do for the Sarahs? We can give them moments, not measuring time "as the world does" but just trusting that a short visit, a gentle touch, a wiped chin, a use of her name, will all have their own worth. We can sit with them, cover them if they are cold, open or close a window, offer a prayer or read familiar scripture, admire their photographs or their newly-done hair, and not run away if they are sad or angry.

The offering of genuine relationship is a spiritual act, whatever the specifics might be. Miriam Hirschfeld, quoted at the beginning of this chapter, says this later in the same article: "As far back as the late sixties, Burnside demonstrated in her early work with demented patients on the back wards of psychiatric institutions that planned nursing interventions such as group work and the use of music, food and touch could make a tremendous difference in the patients' performance level and well-being." To see the truth of this, watch what a friend of mine calls a "million-dollar role play," the movie *Awakenings*, especially the final scene.

The unfairness of life

I did not always find it easy to visit angry male residents, men like Larry. I was more comfortable with females. I tried, though.

Training in the ability to stay with anger surely must be one of the most useful aspects of chaplaincy. Early in my own training, I visited Bella, who was often angry. On this day, she had just been served her supper tray, and she was disgusted with it. "I'd like to throw this mess out the window!" Bella declared vehemently.

I looked thoughtfully at the window. "Don't you think we had better open it first?" I asked.

Bella looked at me as if really seeing me for the first time, then laughed, and we were friends from that time forward.

My own two-year experience as a resident made me sensitive to the trap of being a "good resident." Too often, this required hiding my real feelings to please the parent-figure of a caregiver. It may have made caregiving go more smoothly, but it was not good for my own health – emotional or otherwise. Later, once I became a chaplain, I felt uncomfortable when I sensed that a resident was trying to be pleasant for me, rather than being themselves in an honest way, so that we could begin to develop a genuine relationship.

Certainly the "good resident" trap existed at St. Mary's, as at most institutions – although I noticed that personalities were accepted, eccentricities and all, if the resident spent enough years there, just as the resident of a village earns the right to be her/himself just by living there long enough. Staff earned tolerance for their peculiarities in the same way.

Ideas for reflection or group discussion

- ..... Write for ten minutes without stopping, beginning "When I am old..." Share what you have written.
- ..... Find poems and stories about aging. Share them with the group.
- ..... Find scriptural references on aging. (A concordance – if you don't have one, it's a kind of index to the Bible – will help you trace various kinds of references.)
- ..... Share memories of your favorite old person – and your most disliked old person.

Chapter 4
Sexuality

The tiny red bathing suit of Mr. July

St. Mary's Hospital's Bioethics Committee sat in a circle, sucking their teeth as they passed around a male pin-up calendar. It used to hang on Susie's wall. They didn't approve of it, obviously.

I wondered if they had ever had pin-up calendars of their own. From the looks on most of their faces, I doubted it.

As an only child, I'd had many imaginary friends to keep me company. Even now, during times of stress, I sometimes slipped into this comforting old habit. Confronted by the sour faces of the Bioethics Committee, I conjured up Pauli. Lovely Pauli. She stood barefoot and bare-breasted, smack in the center of the solemn circle of the Bioethics Committee, grinning in wicked delight at her own outrageousness. I tried not to smile, reminding myself that only I could actually see her. Pauli swayed her hips, rosy-brown flesh undulating through her all-natural-fibre grass skirt. She moved slyly towards the intense young physician who chaired this particular meeting with thinly-disguised distaste. Pauli moved closer and closer to him.

Nervously, I wondered whether other semisane adults also had fantasy companions to see them through tense times. Probably not quite like this, I had to admit, watching with fascination as Pauli's feathery lei came within tickling distance of the serious young doctor's nose. I felt the hair on my neck rise when the doctor's long, pale hand suddenly came up to scratch his nose. I quickly banished Pauli for the time being.

I looked around quickly at the ring of faces. Most of them were still absorbed in passing the infamous calendar around the circle, covertly watching one another's reactions. It was a tricky business. To look too closely at any of the muscled males high-lighting any particular month could signify inappropriate interest. Too quick a glance might seem prudish. I did think that Mr. May, of the ever-so-slightly unzipped jeans, got just a fraction of a second more attention than the other models, and it seemed unspokenly agreed by most of the women present that Mr. July in his tiny red bathing suit was most definitely "hot."

It was hard to believe that this meeting had been called in the first place. The Bioethics Committee's august philosophical expertise was generally called upon only for more weighty life and death issues. Even most of the nurses on Susie's floor had confided that they felt embarrassed to be associated with the colleague who had complained to her union that Susie's male pin-up calendar was "poisoning the workplace." But this was, after all, a Catholic hospital.

But Susie, the resident in question, a youngish and generally amenable woman paraplegic, had unexpectedly decided that she was not going to surrender to the "good resident" syndrome any more. She had lost enough already. Her pin-up calendar was just not going to be another of her many losses. She had declined to have it removed from her wall.

I admired her firm stand. It was something to see, this stubborn, frail person no longer quite so helpless. Most of the nurses cheered her determination, but the offended nurse, just as stubborn, gradually brought more and more of hospital officialdom into the fray. Never had a calendar been so well scrutinized by so many.

After examining the calendar carefully, everyone in the circle agreed that it was at worst juvenile. "Inane," someone added. "Meat," snapped the serious young doctor disapprovingly. But not pornographic. Another doctor, slouching in his chair in a bored way, arms folded, looked dreamily into the distance, smiling as if he could recall other far more titillating calendars.

Louisa, the offended nurse, hadn't realized the source of the offending calendar until her complaint had been registered and the union's big wheels were already turning. She was chagrined, as well as taken aback, for she had not expected Susie to have such a committed advocate. But I felt advocacy was the least I could offer, considering I had given Susie the calendar in the first place.

Not everyone might expect that of a chaplain, but the calendar had been only a dollar, because it was already April when I bought it. And it cheered Susie up a lot.

It was embarrassing, I will admit, to have a private joke explode into a public controversy. My friends in the social work department snickered about "pastoral promiscuity," and insisted on referring to me as Susie's "supplier."

Interestingly, though, a nurse who had coldly ignored my greeting for six years now seemed to decide that "church lady" might be all right after all, and actually wished me a good morning one day. And a sweet and bubbly nurse of a somewhat fundamentalist persuasion continued, after the briefest of startled pauses, to be sweet and bubbly, but one day slipped me an inspirational book "to share with Susie," clearly hoping I might consider developing a more suitable type of ministry, given time and enough gentle prodding. It was the kind of time you just live through.

So there had been several conversations with my supervisor, who in turn had dialogued with other managers, and the union people had gone to the Human Rights Commission, and finally the Bioethics Committee had gathered. Sixteen bright, informed people, in a council circle. At lunch time.

I do have to admit that this part of the process was a thing of temperate and reasoned elegance. Countries should be governed so well.

And, finally, those present reached consensus that, in this case, the "good" represented by the resident's rights outweighed the "good" that was the right of employees to a "decent" workplace. The serious doctor felt it necessary to point out that a line had to be drawn somewhere, however, suggesting darkly that we could possibly be starting down a sort of slippery calendar slope. Everyone nodded, fantasizing thoughtfully.

I was asked to return the calendar to Susie, and to report to her the good news. I entered Susie's room to find her staring worriedly into space. I rehung the calendar, then sat down to reassure Susie, briefly summing up the meeting. She said nothing. I looked at her, concerned, aware of how much energy it had taken her to stand her ground. She stared back at me for a long moment, then smiled slowly. I guess I should have seen it coming.

"Thank you, Jean," she began in her hesitant way, "But what... what about next year?"

And from somewhere deep inside, I could swear I heard Pauli laugh.

Keeping sexuality alive

Susie was an attractive, frail resident in her early forties. She was incapacitated by cerebral palsy. Her medical problems were overwhelming, and she tried to compensate for her lack of control over her own body by manipulating and charming others into meeting her many needs. Staff found her frustrating and frightening, because she often experienced medical crises that the hospital as a long-term facility was not equipped to meet, and because she took up much time.

Susie and I connected well. She had a rich fantasy life, trying to make up for the reality forced upon her by doing her best to create her own dream world. She had crushes on the male chaplaincy students, male nurses, and visiting male ministers – always imagining with a right good will that they returned her ardor.

I respected her efforts to keep her sexuality alive, and one day playfully gave her that male pin-up calendar to keep by her bed. I had purchased it in a greeting-card shop. She was delighted, and most of the nurses also got a chuckle out of it. One nurse took offence, however, maintaining it "poisoned the workplace." If she had complained on the grounds that it was sexist, I would have had to admit that she had a point. I generally take my feminist principles quite seriously, and on that score I suppose I did err. In any case, Susie and I found ourselves embroiled in an ethical controversy, because she refused to get rid of the calendar.

Although the nurse was surprised to discover that I was the source of it, she took the matter to her union, which took it to the Bioethics Committee.

And it wasn't over then, either. I promised Susie that I would look after next year, too. I bought her a two-year pin-up calendar put out by the local fire department, with proceeds going to the burn unit of another hospital. I felt this lent it a certain amount of respectability. But to purchase it, I had to attend an autograph-signing evening event and stand in line with a great many giggling, much younger, women. My older daughter, who thought the entire episode was hilarious, accompanied me, which helped a little, though she giggled too.

Would I do it again? Probably. Susie, like every resident at St. Mary's, was a real person, with real needs which deserved to be taken seriously. The calendar, although playful on one level, was on a deeper level a token of respect for Susie's femininity, her three-dimensionality. She was not just a body in a bed; she was a woman.

As for Pauli, whom I thought I had conjured up on the spur of the moment, I discovered later that a Hawaiian goddess of fire and love is called Pele. Go figure.

I don't think I ever prayed with Susie in so many words. She preferred to keep religious matters confined strictly to visitors from her own congregation, who visited her faithfully. I did support her through many crises, both emotional and medical, and was also able to offer support to her mother, who had her own health problems.

Ideas for reflection or group discussion

- ..... Write a paragraph as Susie, as the angry nurse, as the prissy doctor, or as the bored doctor. Share what you have written.
- ..... Role play the healing of the woman who "had an issue of blood" (Luke 8, 40-48). What connections do you see with Susie?
- ..... Have you ever felt discriminated against because of something you could not change? What hurt? What helped?

Chapter 5
Other ethical issues

Beyond the pin-up calendar

The calendar episode was laughable in some ways, but it does illustrate how seriously the hospital took ethical matters. Although the calendar crisis was an unusual use of the Bioethics Committee, the Committee was often convened to deal with more life-and-death questions.

Choosing to die

Twice while I was at St. Mary's, residents with gangrenous limbs refused amputation. There was much unrest among staff, who felt that this should not be a choice. After the situation had been reviewed by the Bioethics Committee – which each time decided in favor of resident autonomy – although the resident's situation didn't change, tension was eased among staff. First, because they felt their concern had been heard; second, because the situation was now clear rather than confused.

Because of the unpleasantness of changing dressings on such residents and the sickly odor of gangrene, these two residents had to be moved to private rooms.

It's strange how ordinary life goes on in the midst of horrific circumstances. I sat with one such resident every morning until she died, a woman with gangrene in both feet, hoping to offer some support. Although she was glad of my company, her choice was that we watch the same cooking show on TV each day – perhaps to bring to mind other, more pleasant odors, as well as less frightening, more ordinary activities than dying. Our conversation, try as I might to take it to a more urgent level, was mostly about garlic, which she held in high esteem.

Although she didn't talk to me at any length about anything deeper, her distraught daughter was a religious woman who later asked me to officiate at her mother's funeral. There was some confusion in the daughter's mind about a plaque she had once seen of the prayer of St. Teresa of Avila which begins, "Christ has no body now on earth , but yours, No hands but yours, No feet but yours..." She assured me several times that Christ had a special use for her mother's feet. Each time I would pray to be delivered from the hysterical and unseemly laughter that welled up whenever she returned to her unique interpretation. She wanted me to work this theme into the funeral, but I managed to avoid it.

(The other time I recall this particular kind of discomfort was when I was with a bereaved man whose friend had died. He told me that his friend's widow had asked him to be a "polar bear." After a while, I realized that he meant "pallbearer." I thought it was a slip of the tongue, until he said it again. I think I excused myself to go to the washroom, where I could let my laughter out.)

Living wills and Health Care Directives

In continuing care, there were sometimes questions around nutrition and hydration. When a resident seemed to be dying – and this could take a very long time – and refused food or liquids, should nutrition be forced? Some staff felt that not to insist a resident eat or drink amounted to neglect, and felt unable to comply with the resident's desire to be left alone. Sometimes, too, family members were divided on this issue, some insisting that such residents be fed by force, if necessary, or intravenously.

My own experience in palliative care had taught me that the dying process has its own rules, and when a body can no longer process nutrients, forcing food or liquid only adds to a patient's discomfort. It seemed like a good ethical compromise to offer nutrition, and to respect refusal when that was a resident's decision.

Like many other hospitals at this time, our institution's Bioethics Committee addressed the issue of Health Care Directives (HCD). Similar to a "living will," these documents were meant to help residents to be treated according to their wishes during a time of crisis when they might not be able to give direction to their caregivers.

The existence of these directives meant that the sensitive issue of death had to be dealt with head on. Not every resident was comfortable with the idea of making a commitment now as to the medical handling of a future crisis (whether the level of care was to be intensive, maintenance, etc.), but many residents and families were relieved to know that they could avoid heroic measures if they chose. Residents, when they were asked, voiced far more fear of "being hooked up to machines" in an intensive care unit than of death itself. Some physicians, trained to think in terms of preserving life as their only function, had a difficult and angry time accepting the HCD policy. Most of the residents took it in stride, but surprised their caregivers at times with their choice of care-in-crisis. One man, paralyzed and plagued with bedsores for years, chose intensive care. Others, who seemed to have much more to look forward to, clearly did not want to live if heroic measures were to be the cost. Most had definite ideas about what they wanted.

I became a firm proponent of the Health Care Directive policy after an incident when I was on-call chaplain in our emergency department. A woman had been brought in from a nursing home, vital signs absent, and had been resuscitated. My job was to deal with her distressed and furious family. Their mother was in her eighties. She already had late-stage Alzheimer's and cancer. She had long ago made it clear that she did not want her life to be prolonged artificially. But there had been no time to ask her family, nor to find this information on her medical chart. (In fact, most charts did not have a consistent place to record such information, and this was a good part of the push to have an HCD document for each resident, kept always in the same part of each chart.) The emergency staff did what they had been trained to do, and revived her. She was removed to the intensive care unit, where it soon became clear that she could not live on her own. When treatment was withdrawn and she was finally allowed to die, it was a much more difficult and painful thing for her and for her family than her natural death would have been.

Vigil with the dying

Many of the nurses had worked in long-term care for 20 or more years. They remembered a time when some of the Sisters had actually lived on site, and were always available to sit with a dying person, day or night. Some of these nurses expected me to be available in the same way.

At first I rebelled inwardly that I should be expected to sit for hours when I had many other things to do. Over time I became wise enough to find ways to meet this need in my own way, through frequent "checking-in" and by sitting for half an hour at a time as often as I could. These half-hours were educational. I realized that most of the nurses cared deeply for their charges, and would often stop by for a look, a word, or a prayer with them. Their own stress was eased by seeing me do what they were too busy to do themselves. Through snippets of conversation during their visits we came to know one another better.

Family members were comforted and reassured in the same way, just to know that someone was there with the person they loved. When family preferred to conduct their own vigil, they were still often glad of a break so that they could go for tea or a bite to eat. When they were facing their first experience of this kind, they were sometimes glad just to speak with someone who was familiar with it, someone who could encourage them to speak with the dying (and apparently unaware) resident in a natural way. This was also often a time when an offer of prayer was appreciated, an honest prayer which collected the concerns and feelings which had been expressed. Sometimes – often – there were tears, but also an easing of the heart.

Sifting through the jewels of life

Story was important, and in its own way, prayer. Story was memorial and appreciation and lamentation. Looking back over personal stories in the company of a reverently interested listener was a valued ritual for many of the residents – especially, in my experience, the women. Those with memory problems sometimes told the same story again and again. Although I sometimes felt frustrated with this need to repeat, I chose to believe that each telling had some merit, either because the resident was still working on integrating that story into herself, or because there was something she was trying to tell me that I still didn't "get." I suspect that the process was more akin to a woman sifting through an old jewelry box, showing her favorite pieces again and again to a daughter. Sometimes I wrote down the story as it was being told, with the storyteller's permission. This not only showed that I valued the story, it honored the need all of us have to leave something of our lives behind.

Often these "treasures" were about relationships or the meaning of life. With Mary, at 91, the gems she wanted to share were theological. Although an Anglican, Mary attended every service offered at St. Mary's, and so was in chapel almost daily. She found the infirmity and losses of age a great burden, and spoke often of the many children she had taught at Sunday School. She remembered with pride that every child in her neighborhood had called her "Granny," and come to her with their troubles, some of them quite serious. But the stories I heard most often had to do with her understanding of God, and how she had passed her faith on to others. Like many elders, she felt strongly that it was high time we all understood that "there is only one God." Distilled wisdom.

Ministry in continuing care was a rich and multilayered experience, with the serious and the absurd all mixed up together, like the rest of life. What made ministry heart-lifting (as well as sometimes heart-stopping) was not the dedicated chapel space, although that was a lovely luxury, but just slowing down enough to get to know each individual as a separate and unique person. When I first entered St. Mary's and saw the many wheelchairs lining the halls, their occupants silent or babbling to keep themselves company, I felt profound dismay. And yet, after I got to know names and histories and idiosyncrasies, after I began to really know each person, my first impression fell away. I kept it in mind, though, so I could relate understandingly to new residents and their families.

I did sometimes think that carved over the entrance should be the words, "Slow down, all ye who enter here." Slow down, and just be with.

Ideas for reflection or group discussion

- ..... What things make life worth living for you? Make a list of at least a dozen things... even little ones like having a cup of coffee in the morning. Now start crossing off those that you could let go of, if you had to. Where do you come to an end?

- ..... Do you have a living will or a Health Care Directive? Do you know what they are? If you have one, who knows about it? If you don't, who could you consult about it?

- ..... Is someone you know facing the end of life? How lost are you going to feel when that person dies? How does that affect your feelings about the treatment you would want for that person?

- ..... Role play the situation of someone who has lived long enough, and desperately wants to go, and someone who is willing to use extraordinary measures to keep that person alive.

Chapter 6
Communication challenges

When words fail us

It was not always easy to get to know family members. Many of them visited in the evening or during the weekend, outside of my regular working hours. Sometimes we didn't meet until a crisis occurred, perhaps during the dying process, as I mentioned in the last chapter. As well as offering comfort and prayer, I often listened to stories of the resident in younger and/or happier days. I valued becoming acquainted with another dimension of someone I might only have known as speechless or confused. This story-telling time also helped to facilitate the grieving process, as memories were shared.

I learned that grieving people often have a great need just to talk about the person who has changed so much. They need to be able to represent this person as more than just this "bag of bones," as someone has said, to represent this person in his or her fullness, as if honoring them. Or perhaps just to set the record straight. Or to remind themselves of just who it is who has died. I was glad to listen; I didn't always get to hear about the other half of a resident.

With Tessie, for instance, I did not expect ever to know her in this way. She had neither chick nor child, living alone with only a dog until a broken hip landed her at St. Mary's, where a stroke had robbed her of the ability to speak. But I was in for a surprise.

Tessie

I like sequels. If any one thing more than another has propelled me through life's ordinary devastations, it has been curiosity.

Sometimes ministry to the very old is difficult for me because of all the cliffhangers, all the half-stories. People die, and I am left knowing only a little bit of their story. I keep coming in just as the movie credits are about to roll.

It was like that with Tessie. I remember going to visit her for the first time. She sat on a chair by her bed, and she was mad. She was aphasic, which means she'd lost the use of her speech, but her body language was loud and clear. After 90 years of independence, she had landed in the hospital for three months, and now she was in St. Mary's for long-term care. And she was not pleased at all.

At first, she just looked at me as if she'd given up hope of connecting with anyone, because she couldn't say hello in so many syllables. Tessie had gotten used to being seen as stupid or "not in" because she couldn't speak. It hadn't broken her spirit, though, the way such treatment can. She just looked right back with a level gaze that clearly spelled, "I'll tell you who's stupid around here."

So Tessie sat and looked at me, and I looked back at her, and we sized each other up. After a minute or two I put it out straight that it must be awful to be treated like you can't hear or understand just because you can't make words. She nodded and relaxed. Soon we had communicated, through a kind of question and answer system and her very expressive self, that she wanted desperately to go home and that she was really worried about her dog. Someone was looking after it, but still she was worried.

Later, I checked her chart. It was true. Tessie was being held in hospital by a concerned physician basically because she couldn't speak. Her hip had mended, and her stroke had left her miraculously intact, except for her speaking ability. The doctor didn't see how Tessie could live alone if she couldn't speak, which showed how much the doctor knew, and demonstrated that he had never had to live with a monosyllabic or moody spouse.

"Tessie," I said next day, "It must seem like you're in jail." She nodded seriously. We sat, that day, thinking about freedom and how strange life could be. A stout little cleaning man came in after a while with a feather duster and rubber gloves and fussed away at invisible dirt, just working right around us. Tessie raised an eyebrow at me and smirked, and I grinned back. When he had gone I asked – routine question – if Tessie considered herself religious. She sort of smiled, and gave a *comme ci comme ca* flip of her hand. It was clear that religion was not an issue, but the theological themes of justice and freedom definitely were.

Others on the team also wanted to see Tessie get to go home, feeling like me that hers was a special case, that this was a woman who could manage at home in spite of her age and disability. Together, we persuaded Tessie's physician into planning a conference to discuss the matter, on a date two weeks down the road.

Two weeks can be two years to someone 90 years old and stuck in the hospital. So, in the meantime, I suggested to the head nurse that perhaps Tessie's dog could come in for a visit. Pets were sometimes allowed in the hospital for therapeutic reasons. It was agreed that this might be just the thing for Tessie. The wheels were set in motion for the following week. I went back to tell Tessie the good news, but she was sound asleep. Since she hadn't been feeling too well that day, I let her be and went home to enjoy my weekend.

First thing on Monday, I went up to see how plans for the dog's visit were coming along. Well, Tessie had gotten tired of waiting for other people to make things happen for her. She had died, just taken her 90 years and gone with no goodbye.

I felt angry that Tessie had been robbed of the time she had spent in hospital, angry that her age and her inability to speak had cost her her own good freedom. But she was gone. I would never know the rest of her story – or even what had happened to her dog, which I had somehow idealized into a paragon of doggy virtue.

It must have been two months later that I happened to eat lunch with a social worker I knew only slightly. She was sitting alone. I was also by myself. Over our food we talked, starting with the way winter had long worn out its welcome and moving on to the sad state of the health care system. I began to tell her about the unwilling incarceration of a resident I had been visiting, and its sad ending.

"Tessie Brydges?" she asked.

I stared, open-mouthed, because my lunch companion worked in a totally different part of the hospital. How did she know Tessie?

It turned out that Tessie had been her long-time neighbor. For once I knew I was going to get the rest of the story.

Tessie had indeed lived alone, except for Dinah-the-Dog. And Tessie had vigor and zest and a sense of humor and many friends. She had tended a beautiful garden, sharing roses and raspberries with her neighbors, all of whom had helped her celebrate her 90th birthday last August with a big party. Nice. And as for dying fast – that, it turned out, had been Tessie's stated wish. I listened, delighted to have my memories of Tessie balanced and filled out.

"And the dog?" I asked at last. My companion rolled her eyes. Dinah-the-Dynamo was a "wild and uncouth" dog, a chicken-leg-stealing dog who had cost Tessie a fortune in vet bills because of her many close calls and scrapes, a dog who would run riot on walks, tongue flapping like a flag, till Tessie was all tangled in the leash. And had Dinah been put down, then, after Tessie's death? No, indeed. Tessie's one and only nephew had taken Dinah out west to live with him, and genuinely seemed to care for the dog.

I sighed, then smiled, picturing the unsanitary uproar Dinah would have caused at the hospital if she'd come visiting as planned. In a corner of my mind, Tessie raised one eyebrow, and smirked at me.

Alternative ways to communicate

Early in my training I remember vividly standing by the bed of a nonverbal resident, convinced that I had been given a foolish and impossible task. How could I visit a person who couldn't speak?

That first time, I believe I ran. But slowly, I began to learn – perhaps to remember – another language, a wordless language made up of movement, position, eye contact, a hundred nuances of facial expression, little grunts and sighs, and an expression of high or low energy that is hard to describe, but real.

The first communication we learned as babies was the communication of energy. Remember? Warmth, gentleness, playfulness... Sometimes impatience, or fatigue. We knew these. Words came later. Body-talk and body-listening were how we learned what our world was like – safe or hostile, tender or tough. We shaped our attitudes in response to those messages, growing into childhood, then adulthood, secure and trusting, afraid and tense, or some variation on these. Words became more important as we grew, but it was the energetic communication we learned first that mattered most.

As adults, in face-to-face situations, somewhere between 80% and 93% of our impact comes through non-verbal channels, depending on which study you accept. In a November 1994 article in *pmc: the Practice of Ministry in Canada* ("Making and taking criticism"), Norma Cole McKinnon cited a 1990 study that claims that in face-to-face situations, 55% of our impact is through body language. Another 38% is through paralanguage, which includes rate of speech and how we punctuate and pause as we talk, and our use of and reaction to silence. Only 7% is the actual words we use.

Although at my bedside moment-of-truth I did not have all of these facts and figures, I somehow understood that the biggest hurdle to communicating in such a situation was not the resident's lack of speech, but my own anxiety and discomfort with the silence between us. If someone had a problem here, it was not the resident!

Fear of silence

Silence can be very threatening. We may unconsciously remember times when it was used in hostile or manipulative ways, and we may become anxious. Then we are in danger of becoming reactive, of babbling small-talk, or retreating without meeting the need of the other, as I did on my first brief, red-faced visit.

The resident I visited that day had lost the use of speech because of brain damage caused by a stroke. This consequence of a stroke is called aphasia, and results in various degrees of scrambled communication. Yet there are, in fact, a great many occasions for pastoral visiting when communication by speech is either impossible or doesn't come easily. A resident might be in shock, depressed, or overcome by tears or anger. He or she might have a disease of the throat or tongue, or be on oxygen or a respirator. A resident may have suffered brain injury, be dying, speak a language you don't understand, or be deaf, or very developmentally delayed. Sometimes the resident has partial speech, and this has its own challenges.

When a resident had some speech but was difficult to understand, I learned not to pretend that I "got it" when I didn't. One woman was clear in her mind, but had very slurred, uninflected speech. One day she was sitting in her wheelchair in the lobby of the hospital while I was waiting for the elevator.

A kind-hearted but unimaginative priest stopped to speak with her. "How are you, Colleen? Feeling well?"

Colleen clearly had something on her mind, and tried to express it, but the only clear word was "up." She looked distressed.

"That's good. Have a good day!" said Father cheerily as he hurried away.

I let the elevator go, and asked Colleen what was wrong. "Mmrumpf frumpf up," she replied.

"You don't want to be up?" I asked, since Colleen sometimes got very tired and wanted to be put back to bed.

She shook her head.

I tried again, and then again, beginning to feel anxious about an appointment I needed to keep. And then, all at once I understood. Colleen was about to throw up!

Yes, nodded Colleen, somewhat desperately. I hastily pushed her over to the nursing station so that she could be attended to.

Unable to communicate

If you want to understand what it's like not being understood, you need only visit a place where people speak another language. For me, that happened at the 1995 convention of the Canadian Association for Pastoral Education (CAPE). Its theme was "Beyond Words." The conference was held in Montreal, so that language issues were front and center. A shopping mall was attached to the hotel where the convention was held. Whenever I tried to use my small command of the French language to make a purchase, the salesperson would quickly switch to English – a tiny taste of the frustration and isolation we were here to try to understand.

There were many workshops dealing with the challenges of communication faced in chaplaincy. I presented one of the workshops, and attended others. Each morning began with a liturgy that was almost wordless, yet extremely powerful. It reminded all of us that communication was not just words, and invited us to interact with one another, rather than just exchange words.

I began to think that sometimes we use language as a way to keep one another at arm's length, that it has less to do with our desire for connection with one another than our fear of being overwhelmed by intimacy, by the power of silence. When we do not have ready access to words, yet want to communicate, we have to become aware of one another's bodies, one another's intent, vulnerability, need. We look into one another's eyes; we touch as a sign of compassion or goodwill or self-offering. We become aware of the place of the heart in communication, and that can seem dangerous. Language is only one way we express our thoughts. At times, it can be the most dishonest way.

Some non-verbal residents were cognitively handicapped; that is, they could no longer make sense of the world or understand speech. But they could usually grasp the *attitude* of another, and would often respond to kindness and patience. Some, like Tessie, expected to be treated as less than adult or even less than human, because this had been their experience.

Not a sign of intelligence

Verbal fluency is often equated with intelligence (and therefore with status) in our culture. Pets don't speak (personally, I think that is because they are too smart to speak!); children speak, but are often ignored, discounted, or told to be quiet; and women in any mixed group tend to speak less than the men in the same group. At one time, children were "seen and not heard," and women were forbidden to speak in church.

Because of this connection between speech and perceived power or even humanity, the loss of speech can be devastating to personal self-esteem. It is compounded by the fact that the person's sense of violation and anger from this loss cannot be expressed in words. In addition, much of the literature dealing with the adjustment of older people to institutional life emphasizes communication as a vital factor.

Sometimes I was the one who underestimated a resident, until he or she taught me what I needed to learn. Darren was a man in his fifties, so contracted that even in his wheelchair he was curled up. He did not speak, though I had heard him laugh, and he was a favorite with staff. He was not a chapel-goer. My impression was that he did not have much use for chaplaincy. While he did not repel my advances, he just seemed to wait for me to go away.

But one day, while I was waiting for the notoriously slow St. Mary's elevator, Darren was sitting nearby. It was supper time, and his tray sat next to him on a table, but he could not feed himself. He kept looking meaningfully at the tray, and then at me, until I asked if he wanted me to help him eat. He nodded vigorously, and ate with a good appetite. Afterwards, this man I had never heard speak an intelligible word, said, with so much difficulty that I knew I had received a gift from a gentleman, an unmistakable "Thanks." All the time I had been checking Darren's ability to communicate, he had been checking mine. I'm glad I passed.

After that, I knew I was on Darren's list of "feeders," and we repeated the same scenario several times.

Ina was another friend at St. Mary's who struggled mightily with grief after she lost the power to speak after a stroke. She recovered in most physical ways, but after a month or so in hospital still spent most of the day lying sadly on her bed. Staff was worried about her, and asked me to see her, to (how many times have you heard this?) "cheer her up."

I decided I needed to come right to the point, and told Ina of the concern of the staff. She nodded unhappily. She had retained some ability to write and read (a stroke can rob some victims of the ability to understand written language) and with the aid of a pencil and notepad and "yes" or "no" questions, it eventually became clear that she missed terribly not being able to speak. She had been a very social person who depended heavily on conversation to maintain her relationships.

Institutionalized fairly soon after her stroke, Ina felt paralyzed by the sense of outraged grief she felt like a tidal wave of loss. She also found it painful and humiliating to be overlooked or treated like a child or as mentally slow just because she couldn't speak. We visited regularly, and soon Ina would give me a hug when we bumped into one another in the hall. She also sometimes became very angry (which I thought was great, because she had a lot to be angry about, and it was better than becoming depressed), and would pound her cane angrily on the floor, shaking her head as if she despaired of ever finding one sane person at St. Mary's. She occasionally attended our Friday services, and would give me a thumbs-up if I was the leader and happened to say something she thought made sense, or shake her head sorrowfully if it did not.

When her only son died in another hospital, leaving her almost alone in the world, she brought me his obituary to read, and we hugged for a long time. She lived at St. Mary's for several years. And although I know she was often unhappy, at least she got off her bed and into some of the excellent recreational programs that were offered. She especially enjoyed shopping trips, and would show me her "loot."

I knew it was a release for her when she died, because she had often expressed this wish, but I was glad to have known her, and I missed her.

Listening for the feeling

From the speech therapist, I learned something about the different kinds of aphasia, or loss of language. Usually, it was the result of a stroke. Sometimes persons with aphasia could not speak, but could still understand language. Sometimes, they could neither speak nor understand, and sometimes they made sounds which they obviously considered to be language and waited for my response.

With these residents, as with residents who spoke a foreign language, I learned to listen to and respond to the feeling, to pay special attention to expression of face and voice. Often, this was effective. One gracious Portuguese woman, Lucia, had had a stroke which had caused partial paralysis, but did not seem to have affected her speech, which was voluble, but in a language I could not understand. "Aha!" I thought, and found an obliging Portuguese-speaking member of the maintenance department. I looked forward to being able to converse with Lucia through this kind third party. After a few minutes, our translator explained that Lucia had lost the ability to speak or understand Portuguese, or any other language. So we returned to our smiles, shrugs and gestures – a language in which Lucia was most eloquent.

Another extremely loquacious Italian great-grandmother had a huge and versatile repertoire of expression. She was extremely welcoming, and loved to talk. My role was usually just to listen (which, someone told me, was why I had two ears and only one mouth), registering concern, interest or amusement as seemed appropriate. Occasionally, though, Anna would be overcome by grief, and there was no consoling her.

One day, when she was sunk in sadness, some good spirit told me to take her in her wheelchair to the chapel. I did so. She was a devout Catholic, though she just shrugged when I used in an inquiring tone the Italian word for "chapel" that was one her family had printed on a large sheet at the head of her bed. Possibly, my pronunciation evoked the shrug. At any rate, we went to the chapel. Anna sat, head down, fingering her rosary. The good spirit had followed us there, because I felt moved to go into the sacristy and rummage among the records for some music to serve as background to her prayers. There I found an ancient record of hymns in Latin, and put it on. Anna's head came up, and her eyes filled with happy years, remembering a once familiar world in which her many losses were for a time restored to her.

Ministry without words

Just to confuse things, I encountered residents who could say a few words, such as "yes" or "no." Unfortunately, though, sometimes "no" meant "yes" and "yes" meant "no." Some residents had retained a word or phrase, occasionally of a profane nature. One resident could say only "water," but used it to mean many things, according to various exquisitely nuanced shadings of voice.

As an eager beginner, I sometimes ran to the speech therapist for a wipe-off board and felt pen, convinced that some residents could express themselves through writing, if their cognitive function seemed intact. My flash of brilliance was usually not very useful, as I discovered what the speech therapist already knew and was letting me find out for myself – when speech is lost through stroke, writing and reading are often also lost. In other cases, although the ability to write was still present, the strength or coordination necessary for writing was often absent, and the effort to communicate unsuccessfully only added to the resident's frustration. Gradually, I learned to depend less on words, and opened myself to listen for subtler forms of communication.

Many times I felt foolish, carrying on an apparently one-sided conversation before a skeptical visitor or staff member. At other times, I felt deeply rewarded by the expression of gratitude in a resident's eyes, or the delight as an unspoken joke arced silently between us. One woman, unable to speak a word, nevertheless let me know she considered me her pastor after I led a service at which she was present, merely by her eyes and her smile. Until then, she had just looked blankly at me. The blankness wasn't because she wasn't thinking, but because our relationship had not yet formed. I learned that ministry could be wordless, but it could never be superficial.

Hanging in through tears and anger

Aphasia has more to do with the workings of memory than of damage to the organs of speech. Long-term memory is more easily recovered than short-term memory, or memory of recent events. I was sometimes surprised (and delighted!) to hear an aphasic resident singing a hymn in chapel. I learned that hymns and even poems memorized long ago (when memorization was emphasized in school and in Sunday school) could sometimes be repeated. One very old woman had lost her speech, but retained a very intense gaze. She did not respond to any of my overtures. But one day she looked at me with that fierce look and recited two verses of a poem about being lost in the snow. It seemed to speak volumes about her feelings. She died not long afterward.

Although it is natural for us as humans to reach for words, chaplaincy training in accepting and staying with tears and anger is especially suited to support the grieving aphasic. The sorrow that cannot be spoken can still be expressed in tears. As post-stroke residents tend to cry easily and to be subject to mood swings, the chaplain who is aware of this can be a useful and reassuring resource for staff and family, as well as residents. He or she can reassure concerned relatives that the tears and anger are not only a natural consequence of the damage caused by the stroke, but are also a helpful way of venting some of the pain of grief, and that they can help by "hearing" it as such.

The chaplain (and any other caring creature) may communicate caring by presence, touch, facial expression, posture, position and by the wordless comforting sounds of which we are hardly aware. Through empathy, rather than words, what is needed can be given. Through such ministry, we learn not what to say, but how to be, surely the very heart of chaplaincy. "Cheering up" can seem to devalue or minimize pain, when the naked need is for a companion in it. When "Why?" is the silent cry, the only authentic answer possible is in the presence that offers no reply except a demonstrated commitment not to abandon.

One elderly woman came to St. Mary's able to speak, but almost deaf, as well as blind. When I went to meet her, a staff member told me I was wasting my time, but I wanted to try to connect. I took her to a place where we could have relative privacy, and took her hand in a way that showed I wasn't going to do anything to her (one of the nice things about chaplaincy!), and waited until she relaxed. Then I experimented to find out if one ear was better than the other, and how loud I had to speak to be heard. This was always difficult for me, because I do not have a strong speaking voice, but she was eager for communication, and we both tried hard. Eventually, we had quite a conversation, and I'm glad, because it was our only real one. After that, she was in bed most of the time. I couldn't shout in a four-bed ward, and she died a few months later, but I was glad to have "met" her in a useful way, and enjoyed sharing our conversation with surprised staff members.

Touch, empathy, and our common sense can go a long way towards making up for sensory deficits.

The wonders of touch

As a naturally reserved person, I did not find it easy to use touch in my work, but gradually realized its value when used in a non-invasive and judicious way. I learned that, used gently on the shoulders and hands, touch could enhance a relationship and convey warmth and goodwill. I also learned to heed cues that a resident did not care to be touched, that I could demonstrate respect by showing that I had "heard" this and would abide by their wishes. Sometimes I could find out a resident's feeling about touch directly by asking for permission to take a hand. Sometimes the clue was more subtle: a stiffening or a relaxation in response to my overture.

Sometimes a difficult situation contains its own seed of direction. Ina's lack of speech, for example, provided just the opportunity to bring about the intimate companionship that was needed. We were forced to make much eye contact, to be honest with one another – me, when I could not understand what she wanted to communicate, and Ina with her eye-rolling frustration at both my obtuseness and her own difficulty. We were forced to sit in silence with one another often, to just be with one another. I found myself joining Ina in her wordlessness, using signs and non-invasive touch along with words to convey my meaning. Each of us learned that the other had a sense of humor, and we used it to ease tension and frustration as well as to build our relationship.

I know now that non-verbal visits can force both chaplain and resident into authenticity. With no verbal smoke screen, the visit can go deeper sooner, to reveal any real issues present. Such visits necessarily go beyond "visit" to "ministry," for better or worse.

Reading body language

In my workshop at the CAPE conference, titled, like the conference itself, "Beyond Words," I used a wonderfully wordless scene from the movie *Awakenings*. The movie takes place in another kind of continuing care facility, a psychiatric hospital, and stars Robin Williams as (can you imagine it?) a brilliant and compassionate but shy and inarticulate physician. In this scene, a man who is in love but who is becoming more and more gravely handicapped by his disease, tries to convey to his sweetheart that this is their last meeting.

The scene takes place in a recreation room of the hospital, and one of the young man's fellow patients begins to play a piano. The young woman, without words, touches the shoulder of the disabled young man, persuading him to dance with her, compensating for his disability with her loving young strength. There are still no words – even when the music ends, and she must leave. The heartbroken young man watches her departure from a window.

We looked at some of the feeling responses we had experienced in our own lives when communication was poor (frustration, loneliness, anger, rejection, brokenness) and some we remembered when communication had been good (happiness, connectedness, empowerment, wholeness).

We also used a role play based on Luke 7:36-50, the story of the woman who anointed Jesus with an alabaster jar of ointment. Our role play was quite innovative. Marty, a bald male chaplain with a table napkin draped over his head in lieu of hair, played the woman. Mary, a female chaplain, played the part of Jesus. Another woman, Cindy, played the part of Simon. In spite of laughter, it was touching and reverent. We realized together that the woman in the story demonstrates her "great love" without a word, that Jesus demonstrates his in the same way, and that Simon's disapproval was non-verbal, yet obvious enough for Jesus to ask him about it.

Afterwards, when we debriefed (though not at enough length to satisfy some of the C.A.P.E. supervisors present, who loved a good group session!), it was interesting to hear "Simon" say how isolated "he" had felt, not understanding Jesus' rule-breaking response to the woman. The role of chaplain can require a rule-breaking response, that is, a different way of acting or understanding than everyday or obvious wisdom dictates. Because this can be isolating for onlookers, as Simon showed us, (as well as for the chaplain), I think that I would try harder another time to be sensitive to the reactions of other staff. Live and learn.

Ideas for reflection or group discussion

- ..... Role play Luke 7:36-50.
- ..... How is body language used to express discomfort? Anger? Love?
- ..... Babies and pets speak a language of their own. How do we understand them?
- ..... Silence is also part of language. When is it hurtful? Healing?

Chapter 7
Multicultural realities

Hear, O Israel, the Lord our God is One

Naomi and Ruth

The first thing I noticed about Naomi was that she was unusually pretty. A portrait on her bedside table testified that she had once been beautiful. The unpredictable ravages of Multiple Sclerosis had, in her case, meant gradual shrinking and freezing up of her once lovely face and body. Only her eyes still had movement, and in them was a desperation and anger that made my words of welcome stick in my throat.

According to her chart, Naomi was Jewish. As my first Jewish resident, she presented a special challenge. What were the do's and don'ts of ministry to a Jewish resident? Naomi had no family, other than her non-Jewish husband, Lewis. Her beloved father had brought her up alone, following the death of her mother in childbirth. He had died three years before Naomi's admission. His portrait, too, was on Naomi's bedside table. When I asked her about him, her eyes filled with tears, and she turned her head away.

Lewis was everything to Naomi, but as her health deteriorated, so did their marriage. It was rumored that he had been abusive on her occasional visits home. Gradually, his visits came further and further apart, and eventually stopped altogether. He just disappeared from Naomi's life.

Naomi had never been very responsive to staff overtures, but when Lewis left, she became more mutely furious than ever. No one seemed to be able to reach past her anger to connect with her. It was as though she felt betrayed by the whole human race. Everyday remarks felt inane in the face of her sad rage. Every so often, someone would come up with another possible avenue of human contact. It was known that Naomi had once loved beautiful clothes, and she was given a TV which was kept tuned to a fashion channel. I brought her in one of my daughter's outgrown Barbie dolls, dressed in a gorgeous gown, and laid her beside Naomi's pillow. It was hard to read her response, but it struck me as uncomfortably like contempt. I felt ashamed, but left the doll with her anyway, in case I was mistaken. It seemed important to let her know that we cared about her, that she was recognized as a human being with personal likes and dislikes, that she was not just another resident with multiple sclerosis.

The one encounter I had with her that felt like authentic ministry occurred one day when I had taken her for a wheelchair ride around the block. At that time, Lewis was still visiting occasionally, and Naomi was sometimes in good spirits. This was one of her more responsive days. As I pushed, I brought up the loss of her father, in the context of remembering him in prayer, as faithful Jews do. She looked as though she liked this idea. I asked her if she would like me to pray with her the only Jewish prayer I knew, the Shema. She agreed, and out on the sidewalk of a busy street on a hot August day, I began, "Hear, O Israel, the Lord our God is one God..."

I felt moved, and Naomi had tears in her eyes. But after Lewis left for good, she began to look at me as though I, too, had betrayed her, and I think I did, because eventually I gave up trying to reach her.

It began to seem that Naomi was willing herself to die. She would become critically ill, so that death seemed mere hours away, but then would recover, as though she lacked the strength to push herself over the brink. By then I knew that Naomi had not been raised as a Jew, although she was one by birth. But neither had she embraced any other faith, and it seemed important to try to honor her birthright by making sure the Holy Society (Hevrah Kadisha) of a local synagogue would be called at her death, to bathe and ritually cleanse her body (Taharah). A Jewish friend who belonged to this congregation agreed that this would be good, and so this intention was duly charted.

Even after a distant aunt called during one of Naomi's many crises to inform staff that Naomi's body was to be "donated to medical science," it seems that the notation about a proper Jewish ritual remained on the chart. And apparently the Lord of the Universe wasn't about to lose sight of Naomi – even though we had only perhaps three Jewish residents in my nine years at St. Mary's, eventually a second Jewish resident was installed as Naomi's roommate. This second resident, wary and silent after many years in concentration camps, had a very close Orthodox Jewish family: a pearl of a daughter, two elfin granddaughters, and a son-in-law. The son-in-law, a brilliant and volatile man, was extremely protective of his mother-in-law, Ruth (wouldn't you know it?), and called to ask me to make sure Ruth was never taken to Christian services or Christmas events. Every morning, he came in to recite prayers at Ruth's bedside. Naomi, of course, was there too, listening.

Naomi was still living when I left St. Mary's, but died not long after. My Jewish friend told me, during one of our infrequent visits, that when Naomi did die, the Holy Society (also called the Burial Society) was immediately called. She knew this for sure, because she had been one of those called. She explained that it was customary to tell stories about the life of the person being prepared for burial, and because of our connection she was able to honor this part of the ritual. Naomi had a small but proper Jewish funeral the following day.

Jewish law requires that all parts of the body of a dead person (even spilled blood) be buried together. Cremation is not allowed. Even autopsy is not permitted. If Ruth's body had gone to the university medical school as the aunt had instructed, more than one of these laws would have been violated. When I asked my Holy Society friend about this, she said that Judaism held learning in such high esteem that it was possible that giving a body to medical science for the sake of learning might possibly have been permitted. Maybe. We agreed that it was a dilemma for the rabbis to discuss.

At any rate, it felt to me that Naomi might have found a little extra peace in having her body lovingly prepared for a proper burial.

Blessed are you, Lord God of Israel...

The multicultural context

Chaplaincy, in North America at least, requires ecumenicity in a cultural sense, as well as a religious one. Knowing only how to respond to those of one culture (our own) limits our effectiveness as much as knowing only how to respond to members of our own denomination would do. Just as each major religion (and sometimes each denomination) varies in its approach to illness and death, each culture has its own way of dealing with them. Sometimes the rules or expectations are those of a religion associated with the culture (e.g. Italians and Catholicism). Sometimes they are a mixture of folkways and religion, with a dash of regional or family culture thrown in. An intimidating recipe, but culture and religion are always, to quote the multicultural resource booklet *Caring Across Cultures*, "inextricably entwined." (See Appendix for multicultural and multifaith resources you can send for.)

Educating ourselves in this vast area takes courage and curiosity. The further we go into this forest, the more complex the journey can become. We learn, for instance, that Judaism has three major divisions – Orthodox, Conservative and Reform – each with its own beliefs. We go a little further, and discover that Muslims and Jews share some of the same beliefs around funeral arrangements, including ritual washing, winding in shrouds, plain caskets, all-night vigils, speedy interments, and no embalming. Hmm.

Einstein once remarked that it wasn't necessary to know everything, if we just know where to find it when we need it. An unfamiliar culture, faith or denomination remains that way only until we learn something about it. Sometimes, we will be taken aback, as I was upon learning why a Vietnamese mother of a stillborn baby could not share her grief with her family. Death is a taboo subject in that culture; such an event was considered so unlucky that it should not even be discussed. And sometimes, we will feel wonder – as I did when a young man who works in palliative care told me how an Ojibway elder came to sing a "journey song" to a dying Native man. The Native man's roommate was non-Native and very close to death, but had no tradition to call on. However, his family was with him, and they described later to my friend how touched and comforted they were by the prayerful song, and by picturing the two men walking into eternity together.

Ideas for reflection or group discussion

- ..... Institutions clarify actions to be taken in certain situations by creating official policies. Does your department have a policy to guide staff when a Jewish or Muslim patient dies? If so, become familiar with it. If not, what steps could you take to help to create one?

- ..... Imagine that you have been hospitalized in the Middle East because of an accident while you were traveling there. You can expect to be in hospital for some time. What might be different about your care in ways that could make you anxious?

Chapter 8
Funerals and memorial services

Healing the wounds of the past

Gamblers, liars, and chaplains have at least one important quality in common – they need to be able to think fast and to deal with the unexpected. Not everything in continuing care was straightforward, and I think that might have been one of the things I liked best about the work. The surprises, and the need for creativity. This story, which was originally published in the Summer 1996 issue of *The Journal of Pastoral Care* as a personal reflection, tells of such a time.

Heinrich

Heinrich was a pain in the ass at the hospital. A dialysis resident for years and years, he drove the nurses so crazy with his demands and hostility that after a while they didn't always answer his bell. He had been passed from hospital to hospital, from ward to ward. He was such a royal pain that meetings were held to study how to deal with this man. He swore, he bumped into visitors with his wheelchair, and once he got into the servery and drank some breast milk that had been put in the fridge by a nursing mother on staff. Somehow that seemed like the worst thing anyone, anywhere, had ever done.

The staff called him "hateful" – which was true, but it bothered them to say it, and then they resented him just a little bit more for making them feel guilty, for reminding them of the limitations of their love.

Heinrich was in turn driven crazy minute-by-minute by his body, full of the itch and torment of kidney failure. Welts came up on him, his head hurt, he smelled funny, and he looked worse. Gray skin covered his miserable body.

Finally, Heinrich was moved to a nursing facility for geriatric residents, delivered up to the relentlessly soothing care of the nuns who helped to staff it.

They insisted he was holy and prayed with him – or maybe at him. They threw around holy water like rain and moved in a large crucifix. And Heinrich had no choice but to simmer down, to acquiesce to their determined care and their stubborn insistence on his basic goodness. "Henry," they called him. "Oh, Henry...you don't mean that!" I think he just gave up.

Heinrich's dialysis wasn't doing him much good towards the end, and the medical staff wanted to take him off the machine, but he was openly terrified of dying, and the nuns kept pushing for just a little more time. Still, he finally did die, like it or not, after being anointed by a nervous priest who had heard all about him. Heinrich was asleep at the time, so the rites went quickly and lightly – the priest was very careful not to wake him up. The Sisters were annoyed, because they figured Heinrich had missed the whole thing, but they told him all about it.

When he did die, it was on a Friday night. The Sisters naturally wanted him to have a proper funeral mass, but the whole thing fell between the cracks. No one seemed to be able to get hold of a priest. The funeral home couldn't or wouldn't wait. Heinrich was a public trustee resident, with no relatives except for one sister in Germany. I guess they figured at the funeral home that one funeral was as good as another, and maybe there is some truth in that, but the Sisters were much grieved to find that a Presbyterian minister had been called to take the funeral. There were a couple of phone calls to the funeral home on Monday to try to get them to wait, but they said they couldn't keep him forever. I thought of Poor Jed, from Oklahoma – "It's summer and we're running out of ice" – but I didn't say it. I did say a couple of other things. Probably unwisely.

So the Sisters were upset. And the funeral director was upset because the hospital chaplain – me – was upset at him and had been rude on the phone about the handling of Heinrich's funeral. The social worker assigned to Heinrich in the home was confused as well as upset, because he had been told that the whole thing was under control, back on Friday night. Heinrich's dying was as messy and dark and chaotic as a death could be, but it was Heinrich for sure.

After I hung up on the funeral director, I went to have coffee with a chaplain friend. I guess mostly I needed an understanding ear. While I was steaming over my coffee, the phone rang, and it was the funeral director, who wanted to make up. Perhaps it was wise from a business point of view, but also he was basically an okay guy, just stressed out. We ended up on a civil note, and I said I'd attend the funeral.

That's when the strange thing happened! You know the kind of thing I mean – an event somehow vibrates on another plane of existence, just looking to get into the everyday world and make people wonder where they're at and maybe consider that there might be more going on than they can see or understand. It happens most around birth and death and pain and love – mysteries. Synchronicity, grace, whatever – the experience is always weird, so that you are careful who you share it with, and gorgeous, so you never forget it.

In this case, what happened was that the other chaplain had known Heinrich from another hospital. He knew things about him that I hadn't been aware of. He knew that Heinrich had been the son of a Nazi soldier during the Third Reich, with all the negativity and agony and just plain warpedness of such a rearing, as well as all the guilt and shame of being the children of that nightmare. I had read about the long pain of the children and grandchildren of the victims of the Holocaust, but I had never considered that of the children of the perpetrators.

I felt shocked. I think I went blank for a minute. It felt important to bring this misery out into daylight, to lay it to rest with Heinrich's poor, tormented, welty body. When I reached the funeral home for the service, I took the risk of sharing this information with the funeral director and the Presbyterian minister. I could tell at once that they felt as moved as I did, and the minister, a little guy with an open heart, invited me to share the funeral.

It really felt right to do that, even with just five minutes to prepare, and me a person who likes to write it all down first and practice. But it had all felt like getting caught up in something (willingly, though) and it really took over then.

I looked for a Bible to find readings, and Psalm 88 came out at me from a King James Gideon, the Good Friday psalm with its unredeemed pain and its agonizing questions, all sounding like it came from someone hanging by shaking purple fingers from a cliff over a canyon. "Wilt thou shew wonders to the dead? Shall the dead arise and praise thee?" And then the final word that sums it up like the clang of a jail door, "darkness." I knew I had to read it. It didn't exactly feel like my own choice, and I don't think I've used it at a funeral before or since, but it felt right to read it near the beginning of the service. The minister – who seemed caught up, too – agreed.

I looked for a second reading. Like the feeling after a battle with integrity – triumph and exhaustion together – it felt absolutely right to read the story of the raising of Lazarus, complete with the stink and the dark and the sisters who loved him enough to get angry with Jesus. "Come out!" demanded the modern scripture version I chose to emphasize the aliveness and immediacy of what was happening. And Jesus' command to those witnessing the miracle, "Unbind him!"

And that's how we did the funeral. Four of Henry's nuns sat there, very unhappy at not having a mass and uncomfortable with the odd couple conducting the service. They had carted in another big crucifix, and put a kneeler before the coffin that looked like gray cardboard, and at the end they stood up and sang, "O Sacred Head Surrounded" in their high voices. And then we all shook hands and I hurried out to keep a lunch date.

I don't know why it went as it did. During the funeral I shared out loud the story of what Heinrich had "endured from his youth," like the psalmist, and the nuns looked down at the rug, likely thinking that this should not have been spoken. But it felt like freedom to me, like exorcism and justice, though not wide-angle justice, which would have included how his father got like he did and all the ocean of pain that drowned so many. Still, who knows what the reverberations were? Somehow, when you throw truth out like that into the light there are ripples no one would believe.

Of course, there were still explanations to be made to the Sisters, and these were received with a sort of skeptical forgiveness. One of the nuns did say that Heinrich really did sound like the psalm sometimes, lamenting his past, afraid of his future, and not all that crazy about his present. It must have been awful, all of it. But it did seem at the end as if all his dark energy gathered itself up and ended on a burst of truth like a flash of lightning, so that, just for a moment, we understood.

The pain of personal histories

Each resident at St. Mary's had been shaped by a personal history. Because any institution needs order and efficiency to operate smoothly, an inevitable tension existed between the institution's demands and the need to remember how unique and worthy of respect each resident was. Although the residents needed to be kept clean, safe, fed, and comfortable, they were not babies, but elders with rights as well as needs.

I found it wrenching to realize how many of the women had suffered abuse in their marriages, or as children, or to hear of the sorrow of men and women who had been forced to go to work at a young age when they very much wanted to continue their education. The myth of "the good old days" was forever exploded for me. The lives of many of these residents had been brutally shaped by both World Wars as well as the Great Depression. Many had lost their parents at an early age, or had lost children of their own to diseases the present generation only hears about in history books. Through all this, they had little to help them cope but advice to "keep a stiff upper lip" or to "bite the bullet."

Some had been transformatively wounded by their experiences; some had just been made mean. Sometimes it took time to tell the difference. One man, Gordon, was blind. He had a room on the first floor. He seemed friendly, and enjoyed company. His wife of many years was a resident on another floor. Sometimes I used to take him to visit her. She had Alzheimer's quite badly, but could recognize her husband, and seemed excited by his visits. I felt very efficient, thinking that I could benefit two residents at the same time, and go visit a third while they were sitting together. Only later, through overhearing a conversation between two nurses, did I realize Gordon had been an abusive husband, and that his wife's "excitement" was actually anxiety. Further, she had a "boyfriend" on that floor, and much preferred him to her husband. After that, I left well enough alone.

Unsung heroes

Although there were victims among the residents, there were also survivors, men and women who felt good to be around, who had stubbornly held on to their sense of humor, their curiosity, their perspective. Most of them, like most of us, were a mixture of the mundane and the extraordinary, and did not want to be considered heroic. Most of them loved something or someone, which to me has much to do with spiritual health, and were most alive when talking of their beloved.

Grant had been an orderly in a psychiatric hospital. After a series of strokes, he lay all day alternating between pleas to die and requests for something to eat. He was always hungry, and never felt satisfied, no matter how much he ate. He was not pleasant to be around, so great was his despair, and so bottomless his hunger. However, he had an adopted daughter, Debbie, and when he spoke of her we caught a glimpse of Grant as the caring human he once had been. He had many close-to-death crises, but did not die for several years. When he did die, Debbie and her daughters were relieved, even through their tears. It had gone on too long.

It takes a special kind of courage to continue to offer friendship and assistance to difficult residents. I did not always have it.

Gertie, for instance, had me running for the woods after an assessment during which she made it clear that she did not want to see me again. She was exceptionally nasty to everyone, and seemed to enjoy frightening us away like so many sparrows. Naturally, she did not have many visitors. She had one sister, who did visit weekly. Gertie had been overheard to comment to this long suffering sibling, "Everyone here thinks you're ugly, you know."

But then there was Grace. Grace was a chaplaincy student, very tolerant and very determined. Gertie didn't welcome Grace's visits any more than she did anyone else's, but Grace just kept coming back with her friendly manner and good-natured smile. There was no great spiritual transformation in Gertie, but a relationship of sorts was established, and who knows what healing that included?

Grace was ordained into the Anglican Church a year or two later, and seems to be doing very well with her congregation. No surprise there.

Assessing spiritual well-being

Spiritual assessment is often a hot topic at chaplaincy gatherings, partly because it is such a challenge, and partly because being able to quantify – even to talk about quantifying – helps us to feel safer, more in control. How do we "catch" something as elusive as the spirit? How do we quantify what we understand, even though we can't see it with our eyes? To me, Grant's love for his daughter was evidence that his spirit still lived. He was connected to her. He also responded to prayer, to his connection with the Holy One.

This was the model of spiritual assessment I understood and liked best, that of connectedness. How are we connected to others, to ourselves, to God, to our community, and to the world? Can we, do we, love? It is no easy thing, after all. Just as Heinrich's caregivers were made anxious by the limitations of their love, pastoral caregivers and family can doubt the effectiveness and value of what they have to give, and guiltily resent those whose needs are deep beyond our filling. Nurse Miriam J. Hirschfeld, quoted earlier as the author of the article "Ethics and Care for the Elderly," quotes the Jewish physician and philosopher, Maimonides, to remind her readers that care includes "the problem of learning to accept one's limited capacity to help someone in need." She adds that "we become angry at those who expose our limitations and remind us of our humanity." Yet our humanity is not the enemy, but that which connects us to one another and to the Holy One.

Pastoral caregivers sometimes have the opportunity to "hear" others into improved spiritual health. When I am feeling mean, feeling unloving, I know that underneath the meanness there is usually sadness and anger. If I can express these feelings, especially to someone who listens caringly, I can feel warmth begin to flow in me again. I tried to keep this in mind when a resident was complaining or bitterly castigating some absent relative.

Sometimes, I was asked to hear what was closely akin to a "confession," an unusual experience for a Catholic woman. There was a tender bond, afterwards, between myself and the "penitent" – but I could never remember the content of our conversation, which surely was grace in action. One hour-long "confession" was a story as lively and complicated as any French farce. At the end of it, the man who needed to tell me his story looked at me gloomily. He was 94, and after a moment I remarked that I didn't see how anyone could live for 94 years without getting into a certain amount of trouble. He burst out laughing, and that was the end of that.

Memorial services

Because memorial services and funerals can be such therapeutic opportunities to do grief work, I enjoyed organizing them, and sometimes leading them. Even when a resident had professed no particular religion, families often needed a time to gather and address their relative's life and death. They needed a ritual, a few words, some honest but kind reflection, and the chance to support one another. They needed closure. They appreciated knowing that this member of their family had been valued by caregivers, and so staff members were usually invited to services.

For private services, I often suggested that a photo or two of the resident at happier, healthier times in his or her life, alone and with family, be made available for display. That way, we could all remember that his or her death was only a small part of what we were gathered to remember.

Our chapel was available for such services. This was especially appreciated either when the person who had died had been a long-time resident, so that other residents could pay their respects, or in situations where no relatives "outside" were left to look after such things.

Once or twice, a family who had been on less than ideal terms with the resident asked for such a service. Although there was obviously discomfort and unhappiness, there was also an opportunity to gently address some painful realities – not to lay blame, but to help to put the past to rest, to affirm that most of us try to do the best we can, and to acknowledge that this best is not always enough to bring about what we hope for. Sometimes it provided an opportunity to ask forgiveness, or to begin to forgive, so that healing could also begin. Again, closure.

Acknowledging the realities of dying

We also had a general memorial service periodically for everyone who had died within the past six months or year. It was held usually on a Sunday afternoon, with time afterwards for coffee and conversation. This social time was important, as it gave families an opportunity to talk again about the one they had loved and were missing, an essential part of the grieving/healing process, and gave staff an opportunity to see whether extra follow-up was needed when this process did not seem to be going well. (My worst mistake of the nine years was sending invitations to two families of residents who were still living. Mortified, I not only called them, but paid for flowers of apology out of my own pocket. Ouch.) For the most part, it seemed a healing time for those who responded to our invitation.

I usually issued the invitation in writing, so that details of time and place could be easily recalled, and sent it about two weeks before the service.

A recently widowed friend of mine remarked that a memorial service at the hospital where her husband died was much like those at St. Mary's, but that the homily had painted such an ideal picture of communication between dying residents and their loved ones that she felt full of guilt afterwards. Although her marriage had been a good one, and her husband a man well able to communicate, and even though they had both tried hard to meet each other's needs, his was not a "happy ending." I felt glad that I had consistently made a point of mentioning "up front" at each memorial service the regrets and difficulties that attend most deaths, as well as the graces, so that those in the congregation knew at least that their experience in no way represented a failure, but rather was part of the human experience. Having to pretend that such a painful time had somehow been a good one is extremely isolating, and grieving people already feel isolated enough. And yet, acknowledging the pain, giving it its due, often had the effect of moving us to a place where we could smile at other memories.

The order for one of our memorial services is reproduced in the appendix that makes up the second part of this book, along with information about other funeral and memorial resources.

Not so happy holidays

One of our team projects was an annual Christmas service "for all who grieve." It took place on the Sunday evening before Christmas, and included survivors of those who had died in palliative or acute care. It was not a gloomy affair, although there were many tears, and it was requested again and again. As at our other memorial services, each member of the congregation was given a taper to light following the reflection.

One of the chaplains leading the service (the whole pastoral care team took part) led a remembering ritual, while music played in the background. For this ritual, two chaplains lit tapers from a main candle, and went along the main aisle lighting the tapers held by those nearest the aisle. The flame was passed along each pew. The congregants were then invited to close their eyes, and to be in their hearts and minds with the person they were here to remember. They were encouraged to silently say anything to the deceased that they wished to say: "Thank you," "I'm sorry," "I miss you," and so forth. We did not hurry this meditation. Although there were always many tears, the peace afterwards was profound.

After the service, everyone gathered for refreshments and conversation. Some staff members made a point of attending this part of the service, too. Many of those attending found it a huge relief to be able to speak of their sorrow with those who had cared for their deceased relative or friend.

My initiative for helping to create this tradition was the result of my own experience of the first Christmas after my divorce, and the feeling of isolation I had experienced at "ordinary" Christmas services which focused only on the joy of the occasion. My experience helped me to realize how difficult the holiday season – and indeed all holidays for at least the first year or two – can be for grieving people.

We also asked those attending the Christmas service to bring along a donation of non-perishable food, and the next day took it along to our local food bank. It is healing to be a giver, as well as one who receives.

A typical service order can be found in the appendix, also.

Ideas for reflection or group discussion

- ..... Role play meeting a very "difficult" resident. What is it like to be the resident?
- ..... Recall the last time you were very angry. What helped, or would have helped, in your anger?
- ..... There is a saying that children grow up to treat others as they were treated. How is that true for you?

Chapter 9
Conclusion

Trapeze artists and dancing bears

Keeping the candle of hope burning in the high winds of funding cuts and the bleak reality of fewer, more highly-stressed jobs pushes all of us to new levels of creativity and self-education. The job must be done, and done without the resources and security we have been used to.

The CEO of the hospital where I worked was fond of the image of the trapeze, with its lesson of needing to let go of one thing in order to reach another, in spite of the anxiety and fear that are necessarily part of transition. What lessons does the trapeze artist have to offer us? Certainly, flexibility. Change is inevitable. We grieve what is no more, but then we look to see what remains or what is growing in front of our eyes. What else? Perhaps the fitness, confidence and heart that comes from good self-care and practicing our skills by working or studying... by creating our own safety net. And finally, cultivating a taste for risk, for living and working the boundaries of the health-care system as it trembles and sways.

But while the image of the trapeze artist inspires, it also tends to put the problem (and any solutions) "up and out."

I can relate better to the grounded image of dancing bears, of very earthbound, clumsy creatures responding to the music of the spirit in spite of their limitations, all of us joining the dance in spite of the pull of the gravity, the seriousness of life and sickness and death. Perhaps our institutions, too, need to see themselves as dancing bears, heavy and ponderous and limited, but capable of sustaining life in an organized way. They need to be admired for their aspirations, for making the effort, however clumsily.

The system must change, and is changing. In fact, it has always been in flux, sometimes for the better and sometimes, as now, in a way that is frightening. Yet at its heart must always be the people it serves, its guests. Our challenge is to remember that they are just that – our guests – and to remind others of that fact by the way we relate to them... with heart, with hope, with humor, and with faith in the ability of all of these things to contribute to health.

Appendix

Diseases, illnesses, and disabilities

Alzheimer's Disease and other dementias

Common symptoms of dementia

97% are confused or have trouble making decisions
97% forget names of people and places
87% have problems with physical ambulation
86% do or say things repeatedly
85% have problems completing tasks
85% act restless or agitated
83% sit doing nothing
73% are stubborn or uncooperative
63% talk to themselves or talk nonsense

Less common symptoms

52% have disturbed sleep patterns
50% see things that aren't there
50% are fearful or suspicious of others
18% have antisocial behavior
14% threaten to hurt themselves or others

Helpful hints for dealing with dementia

Dementia is a medical term, not an insult. It is a progressive condition distressing to residents themselves and to their families. Much of it is caused by a decreased flow of oxygen to brain tissue as blood circulation slows because of partially blocked blood vessels (arteriosclerosis).

1. Help ease isolation by trying to include demented residents in conversation by your attitude, smiles and gestures.

2. Don't talk down to the cognitively impaired. Keep sentences short and simple. Communicate one message at a time, then wait for a response. Talk slowly by prolonging the pauses between your words and phrases.

3. Don't speak too loudly. Turning up the volume will not help, and may cause anxiety.

4. If the resident is very emotional (labile), listen briefly to the concern they are expressing, provide some support, and then gently move the conversation to other ground.

5. Sit down; show that you are committed to the visit.

6. Keep visits reasonably short, for your sake as well as that of the resident. Like any important task, such visiting can be hard work.

7. Don't switch too quickly from one activity or subject to another. Don't expect specific facts to be remembered (although you may be surprised), and don't be surprised if the resident repeats the same thing over and over. He or she is giving you what is there to give.

8. Decrease competing sensory stimulation. Don't, for example, fiddle with a pen or a necklace while talking or listening – it distracts the resident's already-stressed attention.

9. Your visit doesn't have to be remembered to be important. Be willing to be in that moment with the resident, sharing a time of appreciating, sorrowing, laughter, worship, peace or anxiety. Give him or her the gift of your whole self for that moment, and accept them in return. Ministry can be mutual, and communication is more than just talk.

10. If you represent a church or congregation, leave printed or written information about services or perhaps a prayer or familiar selection from scripture.

Some "Don'ts" from Alzheimer literature for visitors

1. Don't ask questions like "Do you remember me?" You're there for a visit, not to add to frustration.

2. Don't argue or disagree. If your friend becomes agitated, try to change the subject. If the agitation continues, leave as gracefully as possible, and return at another time.

3. Don't take any outrageous statement or action personally. Such behavior is a result of the disease.

4. Don't visit in groups. People suffering from Alzheimer's disease deal much better with one person at a time. This applies to family, too.

5. Don't be put off if your friend seems to show no interest in you or your visit. Your visit is meant to show that you care.

6. Don't ignore the person with Alzheimer's disease when you are talking to another caregiver or a roommate. Try to include them with a few words, a smile, or a simple touch.

7. If you are a relative or friend other than the main caregiver, offer that person your understanding and support. Continue to ask after the resident, no matter how seriously he or she is affected by the disease. Show that you remember the resident in all his or her humanness and continue to care.

Resources

Alzheimer Canada
National Office, 1320 Yonge St., Suite 201
Toronto, Ontario M4T 1X2
Phone (416) 925-3552
Fax (416) 925-1649

"AlzheimeRapport" is their quarterly newsletter. To be placed on mailing list, write the national office or consult your phone book for the nearest chapter.

Many booklets are available, including *A Personal Care Book*, to be filled in by a close relative, that is helpful to continuing caregivers. Also *Just for You*, a booklet for those diagnosed with Alzheimer's disease, and *Alzheimer Disease: A Handbook for Care*. Both contain realistic, compassionate information, characterized by a quotation from O. Sacks in one of the booklets: "People do not consist of memory alone. People have feelings, imagination, drive, will and moral being."

Books

The 36 Hour Day: A Family Guide to Caring for Persons with Alzheimer's Disease, Related Dementing Illnesses, and Memory Loss in Later Life. John Hopkins University Press, 1981. Available from ADRDA, 360 N. Michigan Ave., Chicago, Ill. 60601

Alzheimer's Disease: A Guide for Families. Addison-Wesley Publishing, Reading, Mass. 08167.

Winter grace: Spirituality for the later years, by K.R. Fischer. Paulist Press, 1985.

Day to day: Spiritual help when someone you love has Alzheimer's, by C. Murphey. Westminster Press, Philadelphia, 1988.

Helping People Through Grief, by Delores Kuenning, has a section on dementia, "Someone She Once Knew," that includes an excellent listing of books, videocassettes and films. Bethany House Publishers.

From *The Journal of Pastoral Care:*

1987, S.J. Sligar, "A funeral that never ends: Alzheimer's Disease and pastoral care."

1989, R.N. Cooley, "Learning from our elders: Clinical pastoral care in the geriatric environment."

1991, J. Clayton, "Let there be life: An approach to worship with Alzheimer's patients and their families."

1992, T.S.J. O'Connor, "Ministry without a future: A pastoral care approach to patients with senile dementia."

1993, P.Y. Clark, "A liturgical journey at Wesley Woods: Worship experiences within an inpatient geriatric psychiatric unit."

Multiple Sclerosis

Multiple Sclerosis, known as M.S., is a chronic neurological disorder of the central nervous system. It is not itself fatal, although symptoms can cause fatal complications when the disease is especially severe. Life expectancy is affected only slightly. There is no cure, although medication can help to control symptoms. It is not contagious. It is unpredictable and elusive, so that diagnosis is not always straightforward. It develops between the ages of 15 and 45, and is much more prevalent in women.

M.S. seems to be a modern disease caused by some by-product of the industrialized world, and is found especially in the temperate zones. It is not directly inherited. Many people live fulfilling lives within the community. Some, bed- and wheelchair-bound, require continuing care. Symptoms vary from one individual to another, and include vision problems, weakness, tingling or numbness in the legs, loss of balance, bladder and bowel disorders, speech difficulty (slowness, slurring), and, in about one-third, acute or chronic pain, often in the face. Mood swings and withdrawal from activity sometimes occur, and cognitive capacity may be affected to a limited degree.

Heat intensifies symptoms. Sensitivity to heat and fatigue are particular concerns for the visitor to keep in mind – as in long visits or sitting in the sun. Since residents with advanced M.S. can become insensitive to the feelings of others, it is useful to keep in mind that inappropriate behavior in this regard is not something to be taken personally. (The same applies to almost anyone suffering from chronic serious pain.)

Residents of long-term care institutions who have M.S. have probably fought a long, hard battle, with many losses, and need support. Since fatigue may preclude chapel attendance, personal visits may be appreciated.

Reference

Living Well with MS: A Guide for Patient, Caregiver, and Family, by David L. Carroll and Jon Dudley Dorman, M.D. Harper Perennial, New York, 1993.

Parkinson's Disease

Parkinson's is most commonly first diagnosed in people from about 45 to 60. It is caused by the gradual failure of the brain to produce dopamine, which is needed for proper muscle function. It does not seem to be connected to race, gender, or geographical location. Nor is it a modern disease. It is not known to be inherited.

Because it is a gradual disease, and because the use of certain drugs prolongs life, a patient diagnosed at about age 60 can expect to live to about 75. Early symptoms include hand tremor and a slowing of movement (bradykinesia), a change in posture and walking gait, unsteady balance, bowel and bladder difficulties, and drooling. Some loss of mental function is to be expected. Residents with Parkinson's must also contend with oily skin (so that washing and shampooing are frequently necessary), very soft and monotonous speech, and "freezing" – a temporary inability to move that can be very frightening to the affected person.

Although Parkinson's is not usually very painful, it is "no picnic." The author of my reference, Dr. Dwight McGoon, who writes from his own decade-long experience with the disease that forced his retirement from medicine, says this: "Probably no other single factor is as important as the stability and dependability of the patient's emotional environment. The more supportive, caring, and loving it is, the more stable his (her) physical status will probably be, and certainly the greater will be his (her) contentment. Nothing seems to magnify disability and despair as much as emotional stress does." It sounds as if there is a place for pastoral care in this scenario!

Reference

The Parkinson's Handbook, by Dwight C. McGoon, M.D. W.W. Norton & Company, 1990.

Communicative Challenges in Continuing Care

There are a wide variety of disabilities that can result in impaired ability to communicate. Most of them result from some form of brain damage, either progressive or acute. Here are a few of the forms (and names) you may encounter. Because deafness and blindness may also result from neurological damage, and because their effects can also result in communication difficulties, I have included them in this list.

1. **Aphasia**

   This is an acquired language impairment resulting from brain damage (usually from a stroke or C.V.A. – cerebral vascular accident). Aphasia can affect all areas of language: comprehension, speaking, reading, writing, and gesturing.

2. **Dysarthria**

   This is a speech disturbance brought about by weakness or damage to any of the muscles associated with producing speech. Understanding is not affected. Chewing and swallowing may also be affected, and drooling may be a problem. Dysarthria may result from stroke or from progressive neurological disorder such as Parkinsonism, Multiple Sclerosis, or Amyotrophic Lateral Sclerosis (Lou Gehrig's Disease).

3. **Apraxia**

   Again, this is the result of damage to the brain. Understanding is not affected (except when it is associated with aphasia), but the resident has difficulty programming the positioning of speech muscles and sequencing muscle movements to produce the desired sound.

4. **Language of Confusion**

Language impairment as the result of neurological damage, often as a result of stroke, sometimes the result of head injury or overmedication. Residents may be unresponsive to their environment, disoriented as to time and space, and have difficulty with memory recall and clear thinking.

5. **Language of Generalized Intellectual Impairment**

Residents speak less and less often, and say less when they do speak. More difficult language tasks, such as those requiring abstract or general thinking and closer attention are no longer within reach. Speech becomes more stereotyped and repetitive.

6. **Hearing Loss**

From 40% to 80% of residents in continuing care may have some degree of hearing loss. The most common cause among elderly residents is a deterioration of the auditory system due to aging (presbycusis – not a denominational condition!).

7. **Visual Impairment/Blindness**

Much of our conversation relies on vision (body language, etc.) A variety of studies indicate that approximately 50% of our understanding of a conversation, for example, may depend on visual cues. Visual impairment calls for more intentional use of auxiliary cues, such as touch, tone of voice, proximity and information – who you are, what you are doing, who else is present, and a clear message that you are leaving now.

When Speech is Difficult: Dysarthria and Apraxia

1. If you can't understand the speaker, tell him or her. He or she may able to speak more clearly, slowly, or loudly. It may help if he or she swallows first to clear his/her mouth of saliva. Speech therapists who used to help residents adjust to such difficulties are not as available as they once were, due to funding cuts, so your help with such suggestions is not inappropriate.

2. When dysarthria is severe, speech may be quite slow and marked by considerable effort. Be patient. Give him or her plenty of

time to speak. Suggest he or she keep it short – perhaps saying only one word with each breath. Allow time to rest, and try to have your conversation in a quiet place, or reduce noise level as much as possible.

3. Unless the resident encourages it, don't try to guess what the resident intends by finishing sentences for him or her. It's hard enough for that person to try to communicate without having someone rub their noses in their disability by racing ahead.

4. A pencil and paper or a communication board may be helpful, as understanding is not usually affected. Written letters of the alphabet may be pointed out to spell a word. Some residents use electronic devices like a typewriter which show what they are trying to "say."

5. Ask the person to spell difficult words, and echo each letter as they do to make sure you have it correct and to convey understanding.

6. Hearing and comprehension are not usually impaired, so raising your own voice, slowing down, or exaggerating is not necessary. It may help to slow down, however, as a way of reminding yourself to expect a slower response. Your relaxed patience helps to create a space for communication to occur.

The Aphasic
(language and memory-impaired) resident

One of the most helpful things we can do to ease ministry of this kind is to deal with our own anxiety, so we can relax and be ourselves. Here are some things that may be useful to you and those you visit. Be aware that energy and behavior may fluctuate following a stroke, and that some times are better than other for visiting. You can always come back another time.

1. Slow down. Let things unfold.

2. Remember to breathe. It is essential to feeling, and feeling is essential to useful ministry.

3. Center. Stop outside the room if you can, and get in touch with your spiritual center. Use a short prayer or mantra. Stop again inside the door of the room for a moment to look around and to allow yourself to be checked out.

4. Examine your feelings when you are with this person. Are you picking up some feelings that aren't your own? Trust your intuition and your innate (but possibly unpracticed) "tuning fork" ability.

5. Decrease sensory stimulation. Ask if you can turn down the radio or TV, promising to restore it before you leave. (Of course, you will already have asked if this is a good time to visit.)

6. Move slowly. It is calming for you and for the other.

7. Be honest. Don't pretend to understand if the other person tries to speak and you don't understand. Let them know you are willing to hang in until you do understand. Perhaps they can repeat it differently or one word at a time, or can spell it.

8. Aphasia is a big problem for those afflicted with it, a tremendous handicap, but humor is important under the right circumstances. You can afford to poke a bit of fun at your slowness to understand.

9. Eye contact at eye level is ideal. Sit down if you can. Your visit will be perceived as twice as long as if you remain standing, and may be more meaningful because of this symbolic commitment to stay for a while. Residents need time to size up their visitors, too.

10. Empathize. Use your sacred imagination to put yourself in the place of the other.

11. Feedback is important. Use your own body language well. Introverts especially might need to remind themselves to show what they are feeling in situations like this.

12. Aphasia and loss of memory are intimately related. Words cannot be recalled correctly or at all. Memories of long ago are sometimes more easily recalled than recent events. There can be comfort in talking about personal history. Songs committed to memory long ago are sometimes accessed, so that a resident who cannot speak can sometimes sing, and participate in worship in this way.

13. Encourage family members to relate to the resident as they have always done. If they tend to speak about the resident as if he or she were not there, try to model including the resident in conversation, and letting him or her respond in whatever way they

can. Remind family gently that good self-esteem and healing are connected. A resident may have lost speech (possibly temporarily, but most speech recovery takes place within a year), but this does not have to mean that a family has lost a parent, or a spouse lost a husband or wife.

The hearing-impaired resident

1. If hearing is impaired, try to find out if the resident reads lips and or uses a hearing aid. If he/she does use a hearing aid, make sure it is on and properly adjusted. Ask staff for help if necessary.

2. Much communication takes place through the eyes. If the hearing-impaired person wears glasses, make sure they are clean and on the resident. Use eye contact (a good idea in any case!) and make sure the light shines on your face. Don't stand in front of a bright light or a window. Light reflecting off your own glasses can make it hard to see your eyes. Bright lipstick makes your mouth easier to see, but only about a quarter of speech is visible on the lips.

3. In one to one conversations, make sure you have the resident's attention before speaking. Tap the mattress or wheelchair to get attention, rather than unexpectedly touching the resident. If you need to move the resident's wheelchair, as in chapel transportation, first make sure that the resident sees you and knows what is going to happen.

4. If the resident is in bed, raise the head of the bed if possible. A resident who is lying down will have difficulty lip-reading.

5. Speak clearly and slowly in normal full sentences. Do not shout or exaggerate lip movements.

6. Try rephrasing your question if you are not understood the first time.

7. Minimize background noise, such as radio, TV, open window or air conditioner. If you are visiting in a ward, perhaps you can pull the curtains around the bed. While these curtains can never shut out all other sounds, they do facilitate at least the impression of privacy.

8. Sometimes hearing-impaired people nod as if in understanding or agreement just to be agreeable. If you suspect this is happening, check it out.

9. Relax. Allow extra time for your visit when communication is challenging.

10. For more help, contact your local branch of The Canadian Hearing Society.

11. If others are visiting at the same time (i.e., family), make sure the resident is included in the conversation. If necessary, explain what you were talking about. Deafness can be isolating, and at a vulnerable time it is easy to feel paranoid when you cannot hear the full content of a conversation, especially if there is laughter. It can help to touch or hold the hand of a hearing-impaired resident when you must speak with someone else in the room; such touching symbolizes connection.

12. Many deaf persons have speech that seems difficult to understand at first, but time spent together (practice) will make it easier for you to understand one another.

The visually-impaired or blind resident

1. Introduce yourself each time you meet, until the resident recognizes your voice. Explain why you are visiting.

2. The impairment is not a taboo subject. Ask if it is total, or whether he or she has some vision. If you try to ignore the vision loss when it is obviously an important fact of life, you are trying to sidestep an important opportunity for authentic communication.

3. The impairment has a history. It is a serious, life-complicating loss. Speak about it in a natural way, unless it is clear that the resident does not wish to discuss it. On the other hand, there is more to the resident than this disability – a family, perhaps a profession, a religious history.

4. It is all right to speak of things that you can see, the weather, the pictures on the resident's table or wall. You can use your eyes to connect him or her to the world for a while.

5. Your mouth matters. Try not to hide it with your hands. Bright lipstick also makes your mouth easier to see – all other things being equal! (Beards don't.)

6. If you must move his or her wheelchair, explain what it is you are doing, and why.

7. When visiting in his or her room, carefully replace anything you must move, e.g. the bedside table or a chair. Visually-impaired residents depend on memory to locate articles or to get around.

8. Large print hymnbooks or prayerbooks may be useful. Check them out.

9. Speak before touching the resident, to avoid startling him or her. Shake hands. This helps the resident to know where you are. A handshake also conveys much about personality.

10. If hearing is also impaired, determine whether one ear is more useful than the other, and speak directly to it. Sit on that side, if possible. Speak clearly and slowly, but not in an exaggerated way. Sensory impairment doesn't need to mean cognitive impairment.

11. Blind residents who are left alone for long periods of time may hallucinate. Your visit provides needed stimulation that helps keep residents connected to the here and now.

About wheelchairs

1. Treat a wheelchair like an extension of a resident's body. Don't lean on it or touch it without permission.

2. If you intend to move a resident's wheelchair (e.g. for chapel transport), face the resident first to indicate your intention. Do not move it from the back without his or her knowledge.

3. If moving a wheelchair into an elevator, turn the chair around and pull it in, so that it faces out through the door. Do not stick the resident in a corner, facing the wall.

4. When taking a resident to chapel in a wheelchair, ask where he or she would like to be placed, if possible. If a resident needs to be placed near a door for some reason (e.g. agitation, weakness or unpredictable behavior), ask a volunteer to sit with him or her.

Worship services

Let there be life: an approach to worship with Alzheimer's residents and their families

At St. Mary's Hospital in London, Ontario, Canada, there is a chapel, low-ceilinged, inviting, and unusual – unusual because there are only a few pews on either side and a huge empty space in the middle. This space is reserved for the wheelchair folk who attend each service. They use this center space for daily mass, for the weekly ecumenical worship services, for the monthly Anglican communion services, for the Christmas and Easter United Church communion services, and for funerals and memorial services. In other words, the Chapel of Our Lady of Hope is well-used. The pews on either side of the chapel are used by staff, family, or walking residents of the adjoining Marian Villa residential home for seniors.

Recently, a letter came from a nursing home chaplain asking for suggestions for appropriate worship services for Alzheimer's residents. I felt challenged by this request to do some creative thinking about some of our own services.

Since St. Mary's Hospital is a long-term facility, and Marian Villa is a residential home for seniors needing various levels of care, our congregations typically consist of elders who are... well, elderly and memory-impaired, confused or otherwise challenged persons, with auditory and/ or visual problems. In spite of a good sound system, large-print hymn books, and the orienting aids of lighted candles and church-like surroundings, I felt there was often a lack of energy at our ecumenical worship services. This lack of life had disturbed me for some time.

I remembered observing my first services at St. Mary's, privately very skeptical of the ability of many of the congregants to benefit. As each service progressed, however, I marveled to see how even quite withdrawn persons were visibly moved at the time of communion at the various Eucharistic services, and again at the Sign of Peace, when hands were clasped and greetings and smiles exchanged. At the ecumenical services, I noticed that music often seemed to have a similar enlivening effect, but I also noticed that although the chapel was usually filled for communion services (though those attending were no longer bound by legality), the ecumenical worship services seldom enjoyed enthusiastic attendance.

Since it eventually fell to me to coordinate ecumenical worship, I began to try to find ways to improve attendance. Volunteers brought residents to services, and returned them to their rooms. Efforts were made to keep chapel lists accurate and regularly distributed to nursing stations and mobility volunteers. Good communication with nursing managers were pursued. Community clergy from various denominations came to lead worship, and organists came each week to provide musical accompaniment.

Still, in spite of improved organization, it was clear that the services themselves lacked life. Among the many books and articles through which I searched for answers to this problem was a small book called *Ministry of Love*, by S.V. Doughty. In a similar search for ways to enthuse his congregation of seniors, Mr. Doughty had discovered that the most successful format for his services involved familiar short scripture passages, familiar hymns, and a time of prayer. No message, sermon, homily, or talk!

Since most of us who lead worship put a good deal of effort into the "message" part of the services, and think of it as important, this discovery was quite disconcerting. One supervisor had even told me that a sermon was as vital to an ecumenical service as consecration was to a communion service. Perhaps this was so in the world outside, yet my experience did not bear this out in our chapel services.

Further reading shed some light on this seeming contradiction. Since the "message" is meant to be largely interpretative or instructional, the logical functions of the left-brain are called into action – functions no longer easily accessed by many elders, particularly the memory-impaired. Yet familiar scripture, music, prayers, and symbols retain their power to touch many of the same people through the feeling functions of the right-brain. This approach matched the experience of those Alzheimer's caregivers who used music, aroma, touch, and other emotionally powerful ways of "reaching" residents long after all memory had failed.

Doughty's plan for a service includes six passages of scripture (with brief comments), three hymns, and a time of prayer, the whole built around a meaningful, simple theme. In addition, I suggest that a carefully read parable or story be used in place of a "talk," allowing the parable to speak for itself with its own metaphorical strength and clarity. It will provide extra meditative material for the less impaired. Doughty maintains that familiar scripture passages offer "...comfort and the steadiness of the familiar (and) will awaken memories and draw residents into the experience of worship."

To this basic half-hour plan, I add the regular use of the Sign of Peace following the Lord's Prayer. So powerful is this practice for enlivening that it seems a kind of sacrament. Its special beauty is that it is a kind of communion which may be used within any worship context.

The latest innovation at the Chapel of Our Lady of Hope involves many of the facets of worship explored here, yet it is a simple one. Folding chairs are now interspersed with wheelchairs, and the people who sit in the pews are invited to "neighbor" those in wheelchairs. In this way, those who are able to hear, see, and follow the service are also able to cue their neighbors by modeling responses, by explaining what is happening, or by helping to find the hymn about to be sung, as well as adding to their worship experience the warmth of community.

Although this change was at first met by some natural resistance, several persons were willing to try "neighboring" when it was suggested. I took a seat between two residents, and was delighted to watch their raised level of interest as the service progressed. It felt almost like a sharing of our energy. There was better, more heartfelt singing than we had enjoyed for many months. The wandering, fidgeting, and speaking out that we had been accustomed to all but disappeared. Best of all, those gathered seemed to enjoy themselves.

One author writes that "preferred activities (for Alzheimer's residents) are those which provide auditory and visual satisfaction at the moment, and don't require recall to be enjoyed." I am satisfied that our services now fulfill these requirements. The really satisfying conclusion for me though is not so much that we have found a way of worship which meets the needs of persons who must work around disability; rather it has been finding a better way for all of us to come together as family, and to go away satisfied.

Reprinted by permission from The Journal of Pastoral Care, (*Summer 1991, Vol. XLV, no. 2*).

References

Ministry of Love by S.V. Doughty. Notre Dame, IN: Ave Maria Press, 1984.

"The memory impaired need activity," Patricia Hladik, in *Geriatric Care Newsletter*, July 1988.

Point-form summary:
A recipe for Continuing Care worship

- ..... Take some time before the service to really connect with the worshipers. Use part of this time to discover favorite hymns, rather than asking during the service
- ..... Have a good sound system
- ..... Speak clearly and slowly
- ..... Use large print hymn books (check list on page 122)
- ..... Use aids to help orient the confused and to provide ambiance (lighted candles, church-like surroundings)
- ..... Provide music accompaniment
- ..... Be consistent in using volunteers for transportation and companionship
- ..... Keep chapel lists up-to-date and regularly distributed
- ..... Prepare a consistent schedule of services
- ..... Maintain clear personal communication with other caregivers (especially leaders of other programs) to avoid conflict (such as over recreation or physiotherapy), and with nurses responsible for getting congregants out of bed
- ..... Use familiar short scripture passages, especially parables, followed by brief comments (2-3 sentences) rather than a conventional sermon or homily
- ..... Choose familiar hymns
- ..... Include a time of prayer
- ..... Celebrate a leisurely Sign of Peace
- ..... Use a simple theme tying the service together
- ..... Don't have a wheelchair 'ghetto' – mix wheelchair folk with others, especially volunteers
- ..... Stick to a 30 minute limit

Sample service

I reprint here one of our services – for Friday, August 3, 1990, to be exact. Each reading is followed by the "brief comments" referred to in the above article. Its theme is peace in the midst of pain.

Opening Prayer

God of Peace, you call us, your children, together to remind us that we do not walk alone, but in the company of many brothers and sisters. As you care for us, so we must tenderly care for one another. Bless us, we pray, with the peace that comes from knowing we are not ever alone, and that we are loved, and called to love. Amen.

Reading: Psalm 25

We turn to God in pain, even as a child turns to those who love it, those who care when it is sad or hurt. Reaching out in our pain is a necessary step to finding peace, because to be in pain all alone is the hardest thing to bear.

The psalm also speaks of contrition and forgiveness. As we are reminded in the Lord's Prayer, God can only forgive us as we forgive others. We do not mean to hurt others, but we do. It is part of living. We ask God to help us to make things right again, to heal relationships so that there can be peace again in our hearts and in our lives.

Hymn: *Tell me the old, old story*

Reading: Matthew 5:1-12

The Beatitudes reassure us that God does notice our efforts to live as children of God, and that these efforts are blessed. We are also reminded that we are not alone, even when we feel alone and full of pain.

Prayers of Intercession

Loving Creator, we ask your blessing on those we love. Thank you for putting them in our lives.

We ask your blessing on those we do not love. Open our hearts to make them more like your heart.

We remember those who grieve. Bless them with your peace.

We ask your blessing on those celebrating birthdays and other anniversaries. May the year ahead be filled with good things. We ask, too, that those who remember special days shared with others who are now with you, may be filled with warm memories and gratitude.

Reading: Luke 6:1-11

"Filled with madness" – what a tortured picture! Those who judge others shall not know peace, as we all know from the times when we have ourselves felt critical of those around us. Yet those who wish to do good, to save and nourish life within others and within ourselves – for our lives are also precious – shall know peace, whatever the circumstances.

Hymn: *Blessed assurance*

Reading: John 20:19-29

Not everyone finds it easy to believe in the promises of Jesus. Some find faith impossible. Like Thomas, if we are honest with God about how hard it is for us to believe, then we shall at least know the peace of honesty. We may even know the peace of deeper faith. We are who we are. God has made us and loves us as we are. As the psalmist says, "It is not we who have made ourselves." God has made us, and does love us. There is deep peace in accepting that truth.

The Lord's Prayer

The Sign of Peace

Reading: Romans 8:31-19

Hymn: *Take my life, and let it be*

Thanks to organist and volunteers.

Benediction: John 14:27

"Peace I leave with you; my peace I give unto you: not as the world giveth, give I unto you. Let not your heart be troubled, neither let it be afraid."

Go in peace, in the name of the Lord. Amen.

Funerals and memorial services

Anyone can officiate at a funeral, wake or memorial service. Neither license nor ordination is required. Some residents in continuing care may have been ill a long time, and may no longer have a parish connection, so that a chaplain is often asked to "do the funeral," either at a funeral home or in the institution's chapel.

For long-time residents, staff sometimes ask for a memorial service, even if the funeral service itself has taken place somewhere else.

The memorial service can even take place at a suitable time in a sunroom or office. Such a memorial service can also be used to remember more than one resident at a time.

These services are a rich opportunity for ministry and bereavement work. (Is there a difference?) Surviving relatives and staff are often more comfortable with someone they have come to know personally in a pastoral role (however inexperienced) than with a stranger (however qualified) at such an important and vulnerable time.

Sometimes a service shared with a member of the deceased resident's denomination offers a nice balance. In that case, you will have a lead to follow. Catholics have a funeral mass, and Anglicans have a prescribed order of service. The ecumenical kinds of services chaplains are asked to lead are usually fairly open to creative ritual – a mixture of familiar scripture readings, prayer, beloved secular readings, and personal reflection. Although personal stories can be an important part of a funeral, they are especially appropriate during a wake. Each service varies according to the needs of the survivors.

In preparation, a meeting with surviving relatives (or with staff, in the case of an on-site memorial service) is a good place to begin. Discuss their expectations and hopes for the service. Getting to know them is essential for the personal kind of service that brings some comfort and closure. This meeting can take place anywhere, but one opportunity is to arrange it for before or after visitation hours (the designated time for visitors to come to the chosen funeral home to pay their respects to the deceased and the family). A room is usually available for such a meeting, and you can take advantage of the fact that the family will have had to gather for the visitation anyway. With your Bible, a pen, and a pad of paper you can make notes: names of relatives, favorite hymns and scripture readings... (Have some suggestions ready.)

Discussion about the life of the person who has died often yields stories that can become part of the eulogy, and helps families to begin to integrate the death into their history. Perhaps one of the relatives (or a staff member) will be willing to do a scripture reading or to speak about the person who has died. Be ready to step in, in the event that the volunteer is overcome with emotion and is not able to follow through. You may have to finish the reading or story together.

Perhaps someone else is willing to play a musical instrument, to read a favorite poem, or to sing.

You might want to suggest that personal pictures be brought to the site of the funeral for visitors to see. Families gathering these pictures together have a fine opportunity to enter into their grieving with others, rather than in isolation. Family and friends may ask your advice on whether children should attend the funeral, so you may want to do some prior reading in this area. Most "experts" feel that children are better included than "protected," if they want to attend. Either way, letters, pictures, and small remembrances can be put in the casket as a loving gesture of goodbye by adults, as well as by children. I remember one visitation where the deceased was a beloved grandfather. Grandchildren surrounded the casket in the most natural way, and the pockets of Grandpa's good dark suit were full of their letters and drawings. It felt like a place of blessing.

When asked for their preferences as to readings and music, families may appreciate your suggestions. Even if it is your first funeral or memorial service, they will assume that you know more about such matters than they do. Many funeral homes have booklets available to guide you. Since you may not have a lot of time to research resources, here are some possibilities and favorites.

Music

Most funeral homes will arrange for an organist to play at least a processional and recessional, and he or she will be glad to consult with you on the choice of music. If the family wants singing, remember that you will have to lead the singing, and that music sheets or hymnbooks will have to be made available for the congregation. Recorded music can also be used. Or no music at all. Some favorites hymns include the following:

> *Love Divine, All Loves Excelling*
> *The Strife Is O'er*
> *The Lord's My Shepherd*
> *For All the Saints*
> *Guide Me, O Thou Great Jehovah*
> *O God, Our Help In Ages Past*

Abide With Me
Amazing Grace
Blessed Assurance
O Love That Wilt Not Let Me Go

If music without a religious theme is more familiar and preferred, something like *The Rose*, or *Bridge Over Troubled Water*, or classical music such as Albinoni's *Adagio in G Minor*, J.S. Bach's *Air on the G String*, or Pachelbel's famous *Canon in D Major* can set the tone for a time of reverent remembering.

Any favorite piece, popular, jazz or otherwise, can be chosen, however unorthodox it might seem at first. Far better that the service be alive and authentic than to be worried about what outsiders "might think." Some modern favorites include *Rise Again*, by the Rankin Family, Elton John's *Circle of Life* (*Lion King* soundtrack), Bette Midler's *Wind Beneath My Wings* (*Beaches* soundtrack), Whitney Houston's *I Will Always Love You* (*The Bodyguard* soundtrack), and *Old and Wise*, from the Alan Parsons Project album *Eye In The Sky*.

Readings, Prayers and Benedictions

Readings: a few; there are many others. (See also pages 116–122 of this appendix, where many of these readings have been printed out.)

Old Testament:
> Job 19:1, 21-27a (I know that my Redeemer lives)
> Isaiah 25:6-9 (He will swallow up death for ever)
> Isaiah 61:1-3 (To comfort all who mourn)
> Lamentations 3:17-26, 31-33 (The steadfast love of the Lord never ceases)
> Ecclesiastes 3:1-8 (To everything there is a season)

Psalms
> 23 (The Lord is my shepherd)
> 25 (To you, O Lord, I lift up my soul)
> 46 (God is our refuge and strength, a very present help in trouble)
> 121 (I lift up my eyes to the hills)

New Testament
> Romans 6:3-9 (All of us who have been baptized into Christ Jesus were baptized into his death)

Romans 8:14-19 (34-35, 37-39) (All things work together for good)

1 Corinthians 13:1-13 (And now faith, hope, and love abide, these three; and the greatest of these is love)

1 Thessalonians 4:13-18 (So we shall always be with the Lord)

2 Timothy 2:8-12a (If we have died with him, we shall also live with him)

Revelation 21:1-7 (Behold I make all things new)

Gospels

Matthew 11:25-30 (Come to me...and I will give you rest)

Mark 15:33-39, 16:1-7) (He has risen, he is not here)

John 5:24-27 (Who hears my word and believes him who sent me, has eternal life)

John 10:11-16 (I am the good shepherd)

John 14:1-6 (In my Father's house are many rooms)

Non-biblical Readings

Any favorite reading or poem will do. My often-used favorite reading is 3 stanzas, from Kahlil Gibran's *The Prophet*, beginning with the line:

"Then Almitra spoke, saying, We would ask now of Death."

Here is another short poem that has been warmly received by a variety of grieving families and friends:

Do not stand at my grave and weep;
I am not there, I do not sleep.
I am a thousand winds that blow.
I am the diamond glints on snow.
I am the sunlight on ripened grain.
I am the autumn's gentle rain.

When you awake in morning's hush
I am the swift uplifting rush
of quiet birds in circled flight.
I am the stars that shine at night.

Do not stand at my grave and cry.
I am not there. I did not die.

Author unknown.

Prayers

- ..... The Lord's Prayer (unless requested otherwise, a must for Christian services for its comforting familiarity and communal nature).

- ..... A litany (especially at memorial services where many are being remembered), with a part for the leader and responses from the congregation. A psalm can be used in this way, or sometimes a hymn. Or you can create your own for any situation. Copies will have to be provided for the congregation.

- ..... A collect prayer, which can have the meaning of "collecting" the needs of those you are with and weaving them into a prayer, as well as the meaning of a set prayer.

- ..... Prayers borrowed from prayerbooks.

Benedictions

And now, may the memory (memories) of _____, and of all our beloved dead, linger long to bring us comfort and hope. May the death of these loved ones be used by God to draw us all closer to God and to one another. And may the God who raised Jesus from the dead grant to us all the knowledge of eternal life.

Amen. Go in peace.

An added "Go in peace," is a pastoral indication that the service is over. Many people who attend funerals and memorial services are otherwise unfamiliar with church protocol, and appreciate being cued when to sit, stand and leave. I learned the hard way not to step down from the lectern (e.g. to offer the Sign of Peace) without making it very clear that the service was not over yet.

A prayer for caregivers

May the God of compassion continue to smile on you as you go about your work of caring for the needs of the sick. May you be blessed in every area of your lives, today and always. Amen.

Or, a benediction from scripture, such as

The grace of the Lord Jesus Christ,
the love of God,
and the fellowship of the Holy Spirit
be with you all.

2 Corinthians 13:13

These are just suggestions. Create, improvise, ask around, read. But prepare. (Or maybe that's just my own anxiety speaking; I have a secret fear of not preparing and then finding in the service that the only prayer I can remember will be a grace before meals.)

An order for a memorial service

Welcome and Prayer
Hymn: *Holy, Holy, Holy*
Reading: Genesis 49:29-33, 50:1-4
Reading from *The Prophet* by Kahlil Gibran
Reading: Psalm 46
Prayer
Reading: Matthew 25:31-40
Reflection
Remembrance of Our Dead: Meditation with Music, Last Words, Letting Go
Reading of the names of those who died over the last six months
Prayer
Hymn: *The Lord's My Shepherd*
Benediction

The names of those who had died were printed on the inside of the service sheet, along with an invitation to stay for refreshments after the service.

For all who grieve:
A candlelight Christmas service

"For all who grieve"
as used on December 22, 1991

Welcome and Prayer
Carol: *O Come All Ye Faithful*
Reading: Isaiah 42:1-4
Carol: *Once In Royal David's City*
Reading: Luke 2:1-14
Meditation
Lighting of Candles
Carol: *Silent Night*

Reading: From Rainer Maria Rilke
Carol: *The First Noel*
Closing Prayer
Benediction

Sample service for grieving persons

To acknowledge the needs of people living with emotional or physical pain of some kind, a number of "Blue Christmas" services have been developed in various locations. Here is one which may give you ideas for developing your own version.

The Longest Night Service
by Jim Taylor

The service has been designed to have three parts.

Part 1 has the least congregational participation. It recognizes that many of those who attend such a service are ill at ease in conventional church services.

Therefore, the first part of the service allows them to be more or less passive, with the presider carrying most of the leadership. (One of the people consulted about this service said, "There are times when I just want to sit back and absorb..."

Part 2 shifts the mood towards more active involvement by the congregation.

In this service, we recommend not having a conventional sermon. Instead, we suggest a series of readings from the Bible, from both the Hebrew and the Christian Scriptures, followed by:
a) a very brief commentary, identifying a significant theme in that reading
b) the lighting of a candle by a volunteer from the congregation
c) a brief prayer.

We suggest lighting candles because their light becomes a sign of hope in this season of darkness. (If feasible, dim the lights in the church to accentuate the light from the candles.)

As leader, you may want to preface this portion of the service by explaining that the Scriptures present a picture. Although all we have time to read in any service is fragments of the Bible, those fragments should, like small pieces in a larger jigsaw puzzle, reveal a coherent larger picture.

Part 3 tries to move as seamlessly as possible from hearing of the Word into enacting the Word. The suggested order keeps words of any kind to a minimum. For that reason, it doesn't include any specific reading of scripture, nor a traditional "Great Thanksgiving" prayer.

Keeping that principle in mind, feel free to substitute wordings more familiar to your own denominational tradition for those shown.

We recommend that the passing of the bread and wine should take place in silence, aside from any words of consecration spoken quietly by each participants passing the elements on. Do not cover up the emotions of this time with soothing music.

The Longest Night

Service

Part 1
Preparation of the people

Call to worship:

Leader: In the beginning was the Word, and the Word was with God, and the Word was God.

People: The Word became flesh and lived among us, full of grace and truth, and we have seen his glory.

Leader: In him was life, and that life was the light of all.

People: The light shines in the darkness, and the darkness has never been able to extinguish it.

Words of explanation:

Welcome to this "Longest Night" service. The name comes from the season – during this season in December, we experience the shortest day and the longest night of the year. But the name also applies to the feeling that a number of us have about this season. It is the "long dark night of the soul," "the winter of our discontent," in which memories of past experiences and the pain of present experiences can become overwhelming.

For some, Christmas Day is the most difficult. For others, Christmas Eve, or New Year's Eve, or the beginning of another lonely New Year.

In this service, we will have some singing appropriate to the season, recognizing that this is not necessarily a season of joy. We will invite you to meditate on the pain and anguish you may bring, and to offer your pain to the Christ child. And we trust that you will find hope and comfort in knowing that you are not alone.

Let us begin our worship by singing familiar Christmas songs and carols. Please listen to the poignancy of the words, as you sing the verses.
Carol(s) choices of:

> *O Little Town of Bethlehem* (tune: St. Louis; verses 1-3)
> *O come, O come Emmanuel*
> *Away in a manger*
> *Moon of Wintertime* (Huron Carol)

Prayer of Confession and Intercession
(with pauses to permit personal reflection).

God, we come to you on this Christmas season, with the pain growing inside us. As the nights have been growing longer, so has the darkness wrapped itself around our hearts.

In this season of our longest nights, we offer to you the pain in our hearts, the traumas that some of us cannot put into words.

God, we come to you as those who have been abused. We have been hurt, physically and emotionally. We have no confidence in ourselves; we cringe away from any threat.

God, we are the outsiders. We are the ones who seem to stand on the edges of any group. We find ourselves always looking in over someone else's shoulders, and when we try to move to the center, we feel as if we are getting elbowed out of the way.

God, we are grieving over what might have been. A death or a loss has changed this day. Once it was a special day for us too. But someone has died. Someone has left us. Someone has moved away. We have lost a job. We have lost a dream, a goal, a cause. We find ourselves adrift, alone, lost in a terrifying new world. This season reminds us of all that used to be, and cannot be any more.

God, we are the victims. We would escape if we could – but to what? We are as afraid of the future as of the present.

The memories of what was, the fears of what may be, stifle us. All around us we hear the sounds of celebration, the jingle of cash registers, the rustle of wrapping paper. But some of us have nothing we can give, and some of us have no one to give anything to. This is our longest night, Lord. Please be near us tonight. We ask it in Jesus' name.

Pause for individual reflection:

Assurance of acceptance by God:

Carol:

In the Bleak Midwinter (verses 1-2 only)

Part 2
Hearing the Word of God for our time, our place

Choose no more than four of the following readings

Reading: Matthew 22:1-10 or Luke 14:15-24 (The Wedding Feast, in which all the outsiders were gathered in)

Comment: This story offers hope for those who have no one to invite them in. It reminds us that in God's divine order, no one is excluded; all are invited.

Invitation: Would one of you, perhaps someone who finds this reading relevant to your own situation, come forward to light a candle?

Prayer after lighting candle: Lord our God, may your fellowship be available to all, including those who feel excluded. Amen.

Reading: Luke 2:1-7 (Bethlehem, where there was no room for them in the inn)

Comment: Jesus himself was no stranger to being a stranger, an outsider, a refugee.

Invitation to light candle:

Prayer after lighting candle: Lord Jesus, let those who are far from home, those who are strangers, feel that they genuinely belong in your company. Amen.

Reading: 1 Kings 19:1-3a, 8-15a (Elijah flees for his life, alone, to the mountain.)

Comment: Sometimes it is only in isolation that we can hear the still small voice through which God speaks to us.

Invitation to light candle:

Prayer after lighting candle: Spirit of God, calm the turmoil in our souls so that we can hear your still small voice. Amen.

Reading: Luke 6:17-23 (The Beatitudes, Blessed are those who weep, for they shall be comforted. Blessed are those who hunger and thirst, etc.)
Comment: This familiar passage reveals that Jesus was well aware of people's sorrows, yearnings, and suffering – and offered a promise of something different.
Invitation to light candle:
Prayer after lighting candle: Lord Jesus, like this candle, bring some warmth and light to those who mourn, who hunger and thirst, and who weep. Amen.

Reading: Matthew 8:14-22 or Luke 9:57-62 (Foxes have holes, and birds have nests, but the Son of Man has nowhere...)
Comment: In his own life, Jesus shared the experience of having no place to call home, no family, no security.
Invitation to light candle:
Prayer after lighting candle: Lord Jesus, you know what it's like to be rootless. Give each of us a way of putting down roots where we can grow. Amen.

Reading: Psalm 22:1-11 (My God, my God...)
Comment: Even Jesus knew the feeling of being abandoned by God, the God whom he had believed in, and of being left alone in his darkness.
Invitation to light candle:
Prayer after lighting candle: Spirit of God, shine like this candle in the darkness, lighting the way for all who feel abandoned, forsaken, and forgotten. Amen.

Reading: Matthew 11:28-29 (Weary and burdened receive rest)
Comment: When burdens get piled on top of other burdens, the load can crush us. In his promise, Jesus offers us help to carry our burdens and responsibilities.
Invitation to light candle:
Prayer after lighting candle: Friend Jesus, we don't ask you to shoulder our burdens for us – just help us carry a corner of them, and we can carry on. Amen.

Reading: Revelation 7:15-17 or 21:1-7 (A new heaven, a new earth)
Comment: Our present world is not how God wants things to be. Those who weep now will not weep later. In this new heaven and new earth, there will be no more need for tears.)
Invitation to light candle:
Prayer after lighting candle: Lord God, your vision seems a long way in the future. Bring your promise closer to us, we pray. Amen.

Part 3
The Body of Christ

Offering: Processing of the offering, followed immediately by the communion elements
Offertory carol: In the Bleak Midwinter (verses 3-4)
Invitation to participate:
Leader: I invite all who profess Jesus as Lord and Savior and who seek to follow in his way and to live in unity with one another, to come to this table with reverence and with faith. Eat and drink for your strengthening, that you may grow in grace and be blessed, remembering that we, though many, are one body in Jesus Christ.

Leader: Peace be with you.

People: And also with you.

Leader: Lift up your hearts.

People: We lift them to the Lord.

Consecration:
Leader: Lord God, we set before you this holy supper, following the command of Jesus, who, the night in which he was betrayed, took bread and blessed it, and broke it, and gave it to his disciples, saying: "Take, eat, this is my body, broken for you."

And on the same night, in the same way, he took a cup, and raised it, and poured it out for his disciples to drink, saying, "Drink of this cup, all of you. This is the new covenant, in my blood poured out for you."

Leader and people: In union with each other and with our Lord Jesus Christ, who gave himself for us and for the world, and in communion with the whole church, we offer ourselves to you.

Leader: And now, as Jesus taught us, we say:

All: Our father, who art in heaven
hallowed be thy name
thy kingdom come
thy will be done
on earth as it is in heaven.
Give us this day our daily bread
and forgive us our trespasses
as we forgive those who trespass against us
and lead us not into temptation
but deliver us from evil.
For thine is the kingdom, and the power, and the glory
for ever and ever, Amen.

The minister takes the bread and breaks it, saying
> The body of Christ, broken for you.

The minister raises the cup, saying
> The blood of Christ, shed for you.

Distribution of the elements

Prayer after communion:

All: For the bread we have eaten for the wine we have tasted for the life we have received we thank you, God. Grant that what we have done and have been given here may put its mark upon us and remain in our hearts, so that we may mature as followers of Christ, and may reveal our faith in our actions, through Christ our Lord and our companion in life. Amen.

Carol: (such as)
> *Go Tell It on the Mountain* (a spiritual, sung by people who knew oppression and suffering)
> *Stay with us through the Night* (from **All God's Children Sing**)
> *Come Thou Long-expected Jesus*

Announcement: about post-worship gathering, if applicable.

Blessing:

Leader: The life of our Lord Jesus Christ, who lived and suffered and died for the sake of all suffering and hurting humans, yesterday, to-day, and tomorrow; the peace of God, which passes all understanding; and the presence of God's holy spirit supporting and encouraging

you, be with you through this season of the longest night.
Carol:
> *Silent Night* (while remaining seated)

Worship resources

General resources

- ..... *Pastoral Care of the Sick*, published by Publications Service of Canadian Conference of Catholic Bishops, 90 Parent Avenue, Ottawa, Ontario K1N 7B1. Contains prayers, scripture readings and rites for ministry to sick and dying Roman Catholic residents.
- ..... *Aha!!! Creative resources for preachers and study*, edited by Ralph Milton, published by Wood Lake Books. While not specifically designed for worship with continuing care residents, contains thought-provoking biblical commentary and many stories and parables suitable for use with this group.

Prayers of faith and comfort

Let nothing disturb you,
Let nothing frighten you.
All things pass.
God does not change.
Patience achieves everything.
Whoever has God lacks nothing.
God alone suffices.

St. Teresa of Avila

Make me, O Lord, an instrument of Your peace.
Where there is hatred, let me sow love;
Where there is injury, pardon;
Where there is doubt, faith;
Where there is despair, hope;
Where there is darkness, light;
Where there is sadness, joy.

St. Francis of Assisi

May the Lord support us all the day long,
Till the shades lengthen and the evening comes,
And the busy world is hushed and the fever of life is over,
And our work is done.

Then in His mercy may He give us
A safe lodging,
A holy rest,
And peace at the last. Amen.

Cardinal John Henry Newman

Prayer for Serenity (especially meaningful to those who have struggled with alcoholism through AA.)

God, grant me serenity to accept the things I cannot change, courage to change the things I can, and wisdom to know the difference;

living one day at a time, enjoying one moment at a time; accepting hardship as a pathway to peace;

taking, as Jesus did, this sinful world as it is, not as I would have it; trusting that You will make all things right if I surrender to Your will; so that I may be reasonably happy in this life and supremely happy with You forever in the next. Amen.

Reinhold Niebuhr

The Rosary

If you are asked to say the rosary with a Catholic resident, or just want to indicate your function by gesturing to the rosary they are holding or that is on their bedside table, you might want to know what it represents. Most rosaries are made up of five "decades" or series of ten beads, separated by a single bead. A shorter strand of beads ending in a crucifix is attached to the larger round. A prayer is said or told on each bead. The Apostles' Creed is said on the crucifix. A "Hail Mary" is said on each of the beads in series, and an "Our Father" on each separated bead.

You already know the "Our Father." Catholics customarily omit "For thine is the Kingdom, etc." and finish with "deliver us from evil. Amen."

The "Hail Mary" goes like this:

Hail Mary, full of grace,
The Lord is with thee.

Blessed is the fruit of thy womb Jesus.
Holy Mary, Mother of God,
Pray for us sinners,
Now, and at the hour of our death.
Amen.

Each decade of the rosary represents a "mystery" or sacred event. The five Joyful Mysteries have to do with the life of Jesus: Annunciation, Visitation, Nativity, Presentation in the Temple, and Finding the Child Jesus in the Temple. The Sorrowful Mysteries have to do with the crucifixion of Jesus: Agony in the garden, Scourging at the Pillar, Crowning with Thorns, Carrying of the Cross, and Crucifixion. The Glorious Mysteries are the most – but not exclusively – Catholic: Resurrection, Ascension, Descent of the Holy Spirit at Pentecost, Assumption of Mary into Heaven, and The Coronation of Our Lady in Heaven.

Some Catholics concentrate on certain mysteries depending on the day of the week, but the ill especially may meditate on whatever mysteries they wish.

The rosary was developed in its modern form around 1425, a time when not everyone could read or have personal access to Scripture. Meditation using the rosary is calming for many people, and the prayers memorized long ago by many Catholics can sometimes still be recited even when all else is confused, a sort of touchstone of the spirit.

Scripture passages of faith and comfort

O Lord, my heart is not lifted up,
my eyes are not raised too high;
I do not occupy myself with things too great and too marvelous for me.
But I have calmed and quieted my soul,
like a weaned child with its mother;
my soul is like the weaned child that is with me.
O Israel, hope in the Lord
from this time on and forevermore.

Psalm 131 (NRSV)

Blessed are the poor in spirit, for theirs is the kingdom of heaven.

Blessed are those who mourn, for they will be comforted.

Blessed are the meek, for they will inherit the earth.

Blessed are those who hunger and thirst for righteousness, for they will be filled.

Blessed are the merciful, for they will receive mercy.

Blessed are the pure in heart, for they will see God.

Blessed are the peacemakers, for they will be called children of God.

Blessed are those who are persecuted for righteousness' sake, for theirs is the kingdom of heaven.

Blessed are you when people revile you and persecute you and utter all kinds of evil against you falsely on my account. Rejoice and be glad, for your reward is great in heaven, for in the same way they persecuted the prophets who were before you.

The Beatitudes, Matthew 5:3-11, NRSV

Ask, and it will be given you;

search, and you will find;

knock, and the door will be opened for you.

For everyone who asks receives,

and everyone who searches finds,

and for everyone who knocks, the door will be opened.

Is there anyone among you who, if your child asks for bread, will give a stone?

Or if the child asks for a fish, will give a snake?

If you then, who are evil, know how to give good gifts to your children, how much more will your Father in heaven give good things to those who ask him!

Matthew 7:7-11, NRSV

When Jesus entered Peter's house, he saw his mother-in-law lying in bed with a fever; he touched her hand, and the fever left her, and she got up and began to serve him. That evening they brought to him many who were possessed with demons; and he cast out the spirits with a word, and cured all who were sick. This was to fulfill what had been spoken through the prophet Isaiah, "He took our infirmities and bore our diseases."

Matthew 8:14-17

Are not two sparrows sold for a penny? Yet not one of them will fall to the ground apart from your Father. And even the hairs of your head are all counted. So do not be afraid; you are of more value than many sparrows.

Matthew 10:29-31, NRSV

The Lord is my shepherd, I shall not want.
He makes me lie down in green pastures;
he leads me beside still waters;
he restores my soul.
He leads me in right paths
for his name's sake.

Even though I walk through the darkest valley,
I fear no evil;
for you are with me;
your rod and your staff – they comfort me.

You prepare a table before me
in the presence of my enemies;
you anoint my head with oil;
my cup overflows.
Surely goodness and mercy
shall follow me
all the days of my life,
and I shall dwell in the house of the Lord
my whole life long.

Psalm 23, NRSV

Come to me, all you that are weary and are carrying heavy burdens, and I will give you rest. Take my yoke upon you, and learn from me; for I am gentle and humble in heart, and you will find rest for your souls. For my yoke is easy, and my burden is light.

Matthew 11:28-30

I lift up my eyes to the hills – from where will my help come?
My help comes from the Lord who made heaven and earth.
He will not let your foot be moved;
he who keeps you will not slumber.

He who keeps Israel will neither slumber nor sleep.
The Lord is your keeper;
the Lord is your shade at your right hand.
The sun shall not strike you by day,
nor the moon by night.

The Lord will keep you from all evil;
he will keep your life.
The Lord will keep your going out and your coming in
from this time on and forevermore.

Psalm 121, NRSV

We know that all things work together for good for those who love God, who are called according to his purpose. For those whom God foreknew he also predestined to be conformed to the image of his Son, in order that he might be the firstborn within a large family. And those whom he predestined he also called; and those whom he called he also justified; and those whom he justified he also glorified.

What then are we to say about these things? If God is for us, who is against us? He who did not withhold his own Son, but gave him up for all of us, will he not with him also give us everything else? Who will bring any charge against God's elect? It is God who justifies. Who is to condemn? It is Christ Jesus, who died, yes, who was raised, who is at the right hand of God, who indeed intercedes for us. Who will separate us from the love of Christ? Will hardship, or distress, or persecution, or famine, or nakedness, or peril, or sword? .... No, in all these things we are more than conquerors through him who loved us. For I am convinced that neither death, nor life, nor angels, nor rulers, nor things present, nor things to come, nor powers, nor height, nor depth, nor anything else in all creation, will be able to separate us from the love of God in Christ Jesus our Lord.

Romans 8:28-35, 37-39, NRSV

If I speak in the tongues of mortals and of angels, but do not have love, I am a noisy gong or a clanging cymbal. And if I have prophetic powers, and understand all mysteries and all knowledge, and if I have all faith, so as to remove mountains, but do not have love, I am nothing. If I give away all my possessions, and if I hand over my body so that I may boast, but do not have love, I gain nothing.

Love is patient; love is kind; love is not envious or boastful or arrogant or rude. It does not insist on its own way; it is not irritable or resentful. It does not rejoice in wrongdoing, but rejoices in the truth. It bears all things, believes all things, hopes all things, endures all things.

Love never ends. But as for prophecies, they will come to an end; as for tongues, they will cease; as for knowledge, it will come to an end. For we know only in part, and we prophesy only in part; but when the complete comes, the partial will come to an end. When I was a child, I spoke like a child, I thought like a child, I reasoned like a child; when I became an adult, I put an end to childish ways. For now we see in a mirror, dimly, but then we will see face to face. Now I know only in part; then I will know fully, even as I have been fully known. And now faith, hope, and love abide, these three; and the greatest of these is love.

1 Corinthians 13:1-13, NRSV

Then the king will say to those at his right hand, "Come, you that are blessed by my Father, inherit the kingdom prepared for you from the foundation of the world; for I was hungry and you gave me food, I was thirsty and you gave me something to drink, I was a stranger and you welcomed me, I was naked and you gave me clothing, I was sick and you took care of me, I was in prison and you visited me." Then the righteous will answer him, "Lord, when was it that we saw you hungry and gave you food, or thirsty and gave you something to drink? And when was it that we saw you a stranger and welcomed you, or naked and gave you clothing? And when was it that we saw you sick or in prison and visited you?" And the king will answer them, "Truly I tell you, just as you did it to one of the least of these who are members of my family, you did it to me."

Matthew 25:34-40, NRSV

People were bringing little children to him in order that he might touch them; and the disciples spoke sternly to them. But when Jesus saw this, he was indignant and said to them, "Let the little children come to me; do not stop them; for it is to such as these that the kingdom of God belongs."

Mark 10:13-14, NRSV

He sat down opposite the treasury, and watched the crowd putting money into the treasury. Many rich people put in large sums. A poor widow came and put in two small copper coins, which are worth a penny. Then he called his disciples and said to them, "Truly I tell you, this poor widow has put in more than all those who are contributing to the treasury. For all of them have contributed out of their abundance; but she out of her poverty has put in everything she had, all she had to live on."

Mark 12:41-44, NRSV

So I say to you, Ask, and it will be given you; search, and you will find; knock, and the door will be opened for you. For everyone who asks receives, and everyone who searches finds, and for everyone who knocks, the door will be opened.

Luke 11:9-10, NRSV

Do not be afraid, little flock, for it is your Father's good pleasure to give you the kingdom. Sell your possessions, and give alms. Make purses for yourselves that do not wear out, an unfailing treasure in heaven, where no thief comes near and no moth destroys. For where your treasure is, there your heart will be also.

Luke 12:32-34, NRSV

Which one of you, having a hundred sheep and losing one of them, does not leave the ninety-nine in the wilderness and go after the one that is lost until he finds it? When he has found it, he lays it on his shoulders and rejoices. And when he comes home, he calls together his friends and neighbors, saying to them, "Rejoice with me, for I have found my sheep that was lost." Just so, I tell you, there will be more joy in heaven over one sinner who repents than over ninety-nine righteous persons who need no repentance. Or what woman having ten silver coins, if she loses one of them, does not light a lamp, sweep the house, and search carefully until she finds it? When she has found it, she calls together her friends and neighbors, saying, "Rejoice with me, for I have found the coin that I had lost." Just so, I tell you, there is joy in the presence of the angels of God over one sinner who repents.

Luke 15:3-10, NRSV

See!
I will not
forget you...
I have carved you
on the palm
of my hand.

Isaiah 49:15

Music resources

Older people have often committed favorite hymns to memory, and can sometimes sing them even when they are not able to speak any longer.

- ..... *Hymns We Love to Sing: 111 Favorite Hymns in Large Print*, published by Wood Lake Books, 1996. Includes such favorites as "Abide With Me," "Amazing Grace," "Go Now In Peace," "I Love to Tell the Story," "Jesus Bids Us Shine," "Kum Ba Yah," "Nearer, My God, to Thee," "Rock of Ages," "Were You There," etc.
- ..... *Songs for a Gospel People*, published by Wood Lake Books, 1987.
- ..... *Catholic Book of Worship III*, published by Publications Service, Canadian Conference of Catholic Bishops, 1994
- ..... *The Book of Praise*, published by the Presbyterian Church in Canada, 1972
- ..... *The Hymn Book*, published by the Anglican Church of Canada and the United Church of Canada, 1971
- ..... *Voices United*, published by the United Church Publishing House, 1996
- ..... *LicenSing: Copyright Cleared Music for Churches*, operated in Canada by Wood Lake Books Ltd. Winfield, BC; in the US by Logos Communications Ltd. St. Paul, MN; and in Australia by Mediacom Ltd., Adelaide, NSW. A great program which also has licenses for hospitals, care facilities, conference centers, synods, dioceses, presbyteries, etc. You name it, they try to get a license. Over 50,000 hymns and songs available. For a small fee you may make reproductions of any material covered by the program – words and/or music – as long as your license is paid. You may transcribe songs and hymns as service bulletin inserts or overhead transparencies; you can even create a songbook specifically designed for your facility. All you need is one original copy of the music.

Reading/Homily idea sources

- ..... *Everyday Parables* – James Taylor – (Wood Lake Books)
- ..... *Sermon Seasonings: Collected Stories to Spice Up Your Sermons* – Wendy Smallman – (Wood Lake Books)
- ..... *Angels in Red Suspenders* – Ralph Milton – (Northstone)
- ..... *And Every Wonder True* – Herbert O'Driscoll (Wood Lake Books)
- ..... *Everyday Psalms* – James Taylor (Wood Lake Books)
- ..... *Snapshots* – Cliff Elliott (Wood Lake Books)

General resources

Bereavement resources

Although life is our focus as pastoral caregivers, death is part of life. Not only are we called on to support families through the dying process and afterwards, roommates and staff also need bereavement support. In addition, almost every resident we meet will have suffered loss, and some will still be dealing with "unfinished business."

Most of us will also have had our own losses. Unless we understand something about how grief works and how healing comes about, especially in our own circumstances, our own grief may distract us from really being with others in similar pain. By at least realizing this possibility, we can better understand our own reactions and avoid getting over our heads when working with others.

There are a great many books on grief, written from many different perspectives. Dr. Elisabeth Kübler-Ross's pioneering work with the dying, *On Death and Dying*, and her subsequent books, have done much to teach us that, while far from neat and predictable, the grief/healing process does have a pattern. Her model of this process has five stages: denial, anger, bargaining, depression and acceptance. Other models of grief, less well-known, give different names to the process, but basically say the same thing: we fall apart, we begin to come together again, we move on.

Anyone can create their own model, and doing so helps bring about understanding of the process. Mine, described in my book *Women in Mourning*, is a three-part model: Not True, The Great Angry Sadness, and Moving On. There is a period of not believing (denial, shock), then a period of sorrow and anger, then an integration of the loss into personal history and an opening to new experience.

The process of grief hurts, and no one can fix it. But a companion in the pain is an act of mercy and a help in healing. We listen, we touch a hand, we care. We stay with. We offer compassion. Although grief-business may have been "on hold" for many years, it is never too late to continue the healing process, provided that the grieving person is willing and able to enter into this difficult and transformative space.

Some of the most difficult times for grieving people are around holidays which include religious celebrations, such as Christmas and Easter, as well as Sunday holidays like Mother's Day and Father's Day. Since pastoral caregivers are deeply involved in such celebrations, it can help to at least mention that the joyful occasion is not (at least at this time) joyful for everyone present, and offer a special prayer for the grieving and their loved ones.

Centering Corporation is a non-profit grief resource corporation that offers a catalogue which includes booklets about dealing with holiday-grief. Their address is

Centering Corporation
531 N Saddle Creek Rd.
Omaha NE 68104
phone: 402-553-1200
fax: 402-553-0507

As for books, first-person stories and books written by people from their own experience are for most people more helpful than textbooks, especially for grieving people. It helps enormously to know that our feelings are not abnormal, and that we are not alone in them. If we want to go more deeply into our bereavement education, Dr. Therese Rando's books are some of the best known and most helpful around. Most bookstores carry books on grief, usually under Psychology or Self-Help.

I'll list some of my favorite relevant grief books, but do go exploring to find yours.

- ..... *Healing the Pain of Everyday Loss*, by Ira J. Tanner, Winston Press
- ..... *Final Gifts*, by Maggie Callanan & Patricia Kelley, Bantam Books
- ..... *Coping With Death In The Family*, by Gerald Schneiderman, M.D., NC Press Ltd., Toronto
- ..... *To Comfort All Who Mourn: A Parish Handbook for Ministry to the Grieving*, by Carol Luebering, St. Anthony Messenger Press
- ..... *Helping People Through Grief*, by Delores Kuenning, Bethany House Publishers
- ..... *Surviving Death*, James Taylor, Wood Lake Books (also available as *Letters to Stephen*, Northstone Publishing)
- ..... *Rituals for Living & Dying*, by Feinstein & Elliott Mayo, Harper San Francisco

General Resources

Expression is a Canadian government newsletter covering all aspects of aging from housing to healthcare. It is published four times a year by the National Advisory Council on Aging, Ottawa, Ontario K1A 0K9. Tel.: (613) 957-1968, Fax: (613) 957-7627. Also available on Internet: seniors@hpb.hwc.ca

Geriatric Care is a four-page newsletter published monthly by Eymann Publications, Inc., 1490 Huntington Circle, Box 3577, Reno, Nevada 89505. A gem – it addresses practical issues in a brief and sensitive way. Minimum order 25 copies monthly for 1 year, $75.

Multicultural Resources

Nursing staff in continuing care facilities may look to you as a chaplain or church visitor for information about the spiritual needs of residents of all backgrounds. It is good to have some sources on hand. (You can always say, "I don't know, but I'll find out and get right back to you.") Having a book about something is almost as good as knowing!

No one book will tell you everything you want to know, but each will shine some light into dark places. For example, one book declares that Muslims (followers of the Islam religion, and situated mostly in Toronto, Montreal and Edmonton, Calgary and Lac La

Biche – honest! – and Vancouver) are buried wrapped in a shroud, and that no casket is used. But an article by a Muslim scholar declares that a plain casket is used. Rather than one piece of information canceling out the other and causing confusion, you are able to tell those who ask that sometimes a casket is used, and sometimes just a shroud is used.

It doesn't really matter, because others will ultimately be looking after these details. But it helps to establish you as someone who knows what she or he is doing – not just for your personal glory, which is nice, too, but so that you will be asked again, when your information might be really important to a resident's care. For example, Muslims and Jews may share similar dietary restrictions (*kosher* for Jews, *halal* for Muslims). If a resident is not eating, and you know that certain foods or ways of preparing them may have something to do with this, staff may be able to have food brought from home or obtain prepackaged kosher meals, acceptable to both Jews and Muslims.

It doesn't hurt to know these things. Language barriers and availability permitting, residents, their families and their spiritual leaders can tell you what their personal customs and preferences are.

Multifaith Information Manual, looseleaf in binder, $23.95 + $3.00 shipping. Send cheque/money order payable to the "Ontario Multifaith Council" or a Purchase Order # to:

> Ontario Multifaith Council on Spiritual and Religious Care
> 35 McCaul St., Suite 200
> Toronto, Ontario   M5T 1V7
> Phone (416) 326-6858 – Fax (416) 326-6867

The Handbook of Burial Rites

> Commemorative Services of Ontario
> Suite 500, 65 Overlea Boulevard
> Toronto, Ontario   M4H 1P1
> Telephone (416) 696-7866 – Fax (416) 696-0227
> Compiled and edited by Louise Winton for Commemorative Services of Ontario, $10, covering everything from Adventists to Zoroastrianism.

Caring Across Cultures (Multicultural Considerations in Palliative Care) focuses on unique characteristics, beliefs, rituals, and care of the dying within nine cultural groups and six major religions. Originally compiled for caregivers in the Toronto area. Not comprehensive, but useful. Cost $8.00 for one copy, $7.50 + postage for 2-19 copies, and $6.50 + postage for 20 or more copies. Send cheque, or will invoice.

Saint Elizabeth Health Care
10 Gateway Blvd., Suite 650
Don Mills, Ontario   M3C 3A1
Phone: (416) 429-0112
Fax (416) 429-8244